T0365964

ASCENSION

AN EFFECTIVE GUIDE TO PRAYING

LAWRENCE DEON HILL

Order this book online at www.trafford.com
or email orders@trafford.com

Most Trafford titles are also available at major online book retailers.

For additional information you may email Lawrence Deon Hill at cfkministries247@gmail.com

Cover artwork: Ezekiel Williams
Cover designed by Robbie Mathews
Edited by Deneen Anderson CEO of MD Writers' Alliance
For writing and editing services, email mdwritersalliance@gmail.com
Coach: Michael Bart Mathews CEO of The Mathews Entrepreneur Group USA
For Manuscript Development services, email wecreatebooks@gmail.com

Print information available on the last page.

ISBN: 978-1-6987-0520-0 (sc)
ISBN: 978-1-6987-0521-7 (hc)
ISBN: 978-1-6987-0522-4 (e)

Library of Congress Control Number: 2020926049

Trafford rev. 04/26/2021

www.trafford.com
North America & international
toll-free: 844-688-6899 (USA & Canada)
fax: 812 355 4082

CONTENTS

FOREWORD

This current dispensation of time has exposed a proverbial opening of humanity's malevolent lexicon. Our history proves we are not strangers to it. The scripture reveals throughout its narrative our exposure to suffering that requires an impregnable faith. Popular pericopes of scripture narrating the journeys of Job; Shadrach, Meshach, and Abednego; the transition of Saul of Tarsus to Paul; and most of all, Jesus, illustrates for us the necessity for a life where faith plays prominently.

The reward for our faith walk is a rich one. Ask Enoch, who by faith never saw death, or those who walked across the Red Sea and water never touched them. Moreover, the word of God implores us with these words, "For time would fail me to tell of Gideon, Barak, Samson, Jepthah, of David and Samuel and the prophets who through faith conquered kingdoms, enforced justice, obtained promises, stopped the mouths of lions, quenched the power of fire, escaped the edge of the sword, were made strong out of weakness, became mighty in war, and put foreign armies to flight." (Hebrews 11:32-34)

But what is faith, without prayer? If faith is the motor, prayer is the fuel. Paul admonished the Thessalonians to 'do it without ceasing.' James taught that 'when performed by the righteous, it avails much.' Jesus said that we should 'always do it and not faint.'

But it is Paul's message to the Romans that should drive us to a more excellent way.

It was 27 years after the crucifixion of Christ. Paul was traveling through the Asia Minor, and having just left Macedonia and Greece, was making his way back to Jerusalem. During this time, he wrote letters for a second time to the Corinthians, whose faith was being challenged, and to the Romans. In his letter to the Romans, which we find in the 8th Chapter of the volume we read today, we find these words in the 26th verse: "the Spirit helps us in our weakness. For we do not know what to pray for as we ought..."

For years I have struggled with Paul's locution. What did he mean? Was he suggesting that we do not know how to pray? Didn't Jesus give us the formula: Go into your room, shut the door, pray to the Father, do not babble...right? Besides, Jesus said that the Father knows what I need before I ask him! So, what did Paul mean?

The journey you are about to take through this prayer module will lay out the blueprint for what is arguably one of the most important parts of the soteriological pursuit. A prayer life is equally as important to your spiritual life as it is to any other part of your life that promotes sustainability.

At its core, prayer is a connection to the Divine. It is the proverbial umbilical cord that provides the nutrients from the One who birthed us during the creation process and leaves a reminder on the bellies of our souls as we grow and develop from milk to meat. Knowledge of its precepts is equally as important as adherence to what drives them. Prayers are uttered by the believer and the unbeliever alike. For while the Christian prays with faith, we also know that there are no atheists who are confronted with mortality who will refuse to pray silently for divine intervention.

Many have taken on the task of scripting an instruction on prayer. But in a field of qualified theologians and expositors of the Gospel, I submit to you that Deon Hill stands shoulder to shoulder at the ready to lead us from the prayers we recited before bedtime, to the supplications we'll utter before end time. Words are unnecessary for testimony when your life speaks. Deon Hill realizes that a transitional shift in the culture will not come through expressions of entertainment and charisma. It takes study, faith, and prayer. He is an example of the change necessary to be admitted beyond the veil.

- Bishop Michael V. Johnson, Ph.D.

ACKNOWLEDGMENTS

To my soulmate, my loving wife, Antoinette, I sincerely appreciate and thank you for patiently waiting for me to complete this book. Your love and support gave me the strength to accomplish the task. You are the wind beneath my earthly wings. To my children Arianna and Keyonna, and my grandchildren, you are the motivation for me to build a legacy that you can be proud of. To my Father and Mother, Leonard Adair, and Shirley Hill-Hall, thank you for giving me life and love. Without the two of you, I would not exist.

To all my siblings, I hope this book makes you proud of me and serves as encouragement for your current and future endeavors. To my entire family, thank you for the love and respect that you give to me. I pray that you are inspired by my Christian walk.

To my church family, Consuming Fire Kingdom Ministries, Prayer Garden Full Gospel Ministries, Message of Christ Church, and Life Changing Ministries of Austin, Texas, thank you for giving me the opportunity to serve as your overseer. I pray that my wisdom and counsel is worthy of your love. To my pastor, Fredrick Anthony of Old Saint Paul Mission Baptist Church in West Memphis, Arkansas, your wisdom, and counsel guided me through some of the most turbulent times in my life; I honor you Pastor.

To Bishop Adonijah O. Ogbonnaya of Aactev8 International, thank you for your mentorship. You are a gift in my life, and you are my Apostolic Father. Words cannot express my gratitude for what you mean to me. Thank you for affirming, consecrating, and supporting me. I honor you Bishop. To Dr. Dwayne Cook, thank you professor for encouraging me to attend COATA (Clement of Alexandria Theological Academy). Without you, I would not have received my bachelor's degree in Biblical Studies. You are truly my friend. More importantly, you are my eternal covenant brother.

To Bishop Michael V. Johnson, of Armour of God Ministries, what an honor it has been since our paths have crossed. You poured into me, supported me, and encouraged me from day one. I appreciate you and Bishop Roger H. Phillips Sr., of Sweet Holy Spirit of Daytona Beach, Florida, for accepting me into the synod of Bishops in New Covenant Apostolic Order. I am humbled by the acceptance.

SPECIAL ACKNOWLEDGMENTS

I want to thank Prophet John Veal for his encouragement. You pushed me to finish this book. Thank you, my brother, for believing in me and speaking prophetically over this book, much gratitude. To my assistant and spiritual daughter Prophetess Latoya Wallace, thank you for your constant reminders for me to schedule time to finish this book. You did not stop reminding me until the work was done. I appreciate all you do for me and our family. You are a jewel; thank you. I also want to thank Henry Abraham who has been trying to push me to write a book for years; thank you, Henry. I appreciate you my brother.

And this last acknowledgement had to be last, because without this person this book would not have happened. To Prophetess Deneen Anderson, founder and CEO of MD Writers' Alliance. Deneen, I do not know where to begin. You are the heart and soul behind this work. Your writing and editing skills took this book to another level. I thank you for your diligence and patience with me. Your spirit, passion, and love for God is infectious! You are to this book what an engine is to a car. Without you, this book does not work! Thank you from the bottom of my heart, and may God reward you richly through this work.

INTRODUCTION

WHY ANOTHER BOOK ABOUT PRAYER?

As I thought about that question, I was reminded of something I read by someone I hold in high regard. If you do not know the intent of something, it is more likely to be used improperly. If you do not know what it was created for, you will not maximize its use. You will not experience the full benefit of what that something has for you. I propose to you, that is also true in relation to the subject of prayer.

If you do not understand the purpose (the reason for which something is designed, created, & instituted), and you do not understand the power (ability, capacity, and potential) of prayer, abuse is indeed inevitable. Therefore, to avoid misuse or abuse, and to provide information, illumination, and revelation for the proper application and use of prayer, this book was written just for you!

Why read another book about prayer when there are so many other books available regarding prayer? Well, that is like asking why read and re-read the bible, when you have already read, memorized, or quoted from your favorite scriptures. Here is the answer to the why: In each book, and with each reading, something is revealed that was not revealed before. Reading this book offers you another opportunity to understand more than you understood before.

By His Spirit, God continues to make known more about Himself, His will, His kingdom, and how we can have unbroken fellowship with Him. Although God is unchanging, revelation concerning Him and His will is progressive. Therefore, our ability to pray must also be progressive and forever-growing. There is always more to learn about God, and how to effectively communicate with Him. St. John 21:25 notes: "And there are also many other things which Jesus did, the which, if they should be written every one, I suppose that even the world itself could not contain the books that should be written."

With that being accepted as truth, no one person, organization, or denomination has the full revelation concerning the uncontainable God! Every book about prayer is needed. Each book, especially this book, gives confirmation or affirmation to the next book. Being divinely inspired, many of the books of the bible were written by individuals who may not have known one another personally. Yet, their writings brought insight, greater revelation, and validation to each other. Likewise, today, each book about prayer brings greater understanding for us to consistently connect and communicate with God.

Prayer is the communication that permits a secure connection to the heart, mind, and will of our Heavenly Father. In that, we can grow in Him. We become more like Him, so that we may lead others to Him. To grow in God, you must grow in prayer. To grow in prayer, you need a secure connection, and effective communication that comes through a lifestyle of prayer. If you pray only when there is a need or some type of presenting trouble, growth may not happen.

Through the great quantity and quality of writings that we have on prayer, we have access to great resources. They enable us to know who God is, and what He requires. Therefore, it takes this book and all other books, written under divine inspiration, to capture the essence of God that enable us, with our finite selves, to communicate with an infinite God.

PRAYER: CONVERSATION & COMMUNICATION

Before continuing to read, pause here and ask yourself what is prayer? Is prayer necessary? Does prayer even work? Now, let us continue by briefly defining what prayer is. In its simplest form, prayer is conversation and communication between you and God. The conversation and communication become more personal and divine in nature when there is a sincere, on-going relationship between you and God. Prayer is the vehicle by which there is an exchange of what is in God's heart and on His mind for what is in your heart and on your mind. Prayer is also a meeting place that grants you access to God's heart, and not just the blessings of His hand.

Know that if your sincere interest is the heart of God, you eventually receive blessings from the hand of God. It is through prayer that you gain intimate knowledge of God and understanding of both His word and His ways. That understanding allows the communication or time of prayer to have greater depth, diversity, and it minimizes commonality.

Prayer is one of the most important forms of communication. That bears repeating, prayer is one of the most important forms of communication! It allows everything within you to come into agreement and divine alignment with the Kingdom of our Lord. Prayer involves the consistent sharing and exchange of requests, information, and instructions. It allows God, through you, to express here on earth what has already been done and said in heaven. Prayer provides the opportunity and the vehicle for God to release from heaven what you and all the earth need.

In the beginning, God spoke and what was invisible became visible. In prayer, you speak and cause the invisible to become visible. This allows the joy, peace, provisions, and protection of heaven to materialize here on earth. If the eyes are the window of the soul, prayer then is the voice of the heart. It is out of the abundance of the heart the mouth speaks or communicates. As a result, effective communication is an important component for effective prayer.

Everything that has life within itself has a way of communicating with other life forms. Whatever God created, He gave it life and the ability to communicate. In some capacity, all people and other species communicate or interact with other people or species within their environment. How, when, and why they communicate or interact is key to their existence. Understand that communication leads to connectivity, and connectivity leads to the ability to grow and reproduce. Nothing within the earth was created to stand alone.

In some way, all that exists is connected, and has the ability and capacity to communicate with something or someone else. In fact, if you eliminate the ability to connect and communicate, then you also terminate the fulfillment of purpose. Therefore, see prayer as a necessity, as it is the lifeline of the spirit just as water is a lifeline to the body. Just as the human body cannot live without water, the spirit cannot live without prayer. A life without prayer is a life without purpose. A life without purpose is a life without power. A life without purpose and power is a life without God!

Prayer is also the strategic means by which we can navigate and penetrate the heavens. Like a sweet aroma, the prayers of the righteous ascend into the nostrils of God and cause a response. Therefore, the act of praying, which is also a form of devotion and worship, should not and must not be allowed to be reduced to a religious exercise or an unfruitful habit.

Prayer is much more than a daily ritual or duty. Prayer must never be limited to just completing a physical act. Prayer is truly a spiritual encounter. Prayer is a meeting place that elevates us up high into the presence of our God. Additionally, it allows Him to descend amongst us. If your prayers do not involve or include God, then they are not the prayers we have been instructed to do. It is important to understand the essentials of prayer, as it assists in understanding the why of prayer.

Why do we pray? Valid question when you consider the fact that God, who created and sustains us all, knows exactly what we need. He knows when we need it and why we need it, even before we know we need it. Why would He instruct us to "pray without ceasing" (1Thess 5:17) and continually make our requests and needs known to Him? Why would He say, "men ought always to pray" (Luke 18:1)? Obviously, prayer must be of vital importance.

Here is another perspective by which you can understand prayer: Prayer to the believer is like the heart to the human body. The heart is the center or innermost core of the circulatory system. Its function is to pump blood throughout the body so that the life of the body is sustained. The heart rate must always beat at the correct rate and rhythm. If not corrected, the body develops symptoms of illness or disease, and death may be the result.

For example, if the heart rate is too rapid (tachycardia), blood flow to organs and body tissues are affected resulting in symptoms of shortness of breath, a racing uncomfortable sensation related to the heart, chest pain, or fainting. If left untreated, heart failure or even death may occur. Additionally, if the heart rate beats too slowly (bradycardia), blood flow to the brain is compromised resulting in fatigue, dizziness, or fainting. If also left untreated, it leads to cardiac arrest and ultimately death.

In other words, abnormalities of the heart lead to illness or death just as a life where prayer is ineffective, inconsistent, irregular, or non-existent leads to a disruption of spiritual flow. The end results are self-centered living, a lack of wisdom & growth, and eventually loss of life. Life without effective, effectual, and fervent prayer is a life of sickness (spiritual, physical, and emotional) which, in the end, results in death (spiritual and physical).

STOP! Close your eyes for a moment. Think back in time, and do a little soul searching. Have any of your prayers been answered? How many of your prayers have been answered? Do you know of family or friends whose prayers have been answered? Truly search your heart and answer honestly: Does prayer really work, and is it important?

PRAYER: QUINTESSENTIAL FOR BELIEVERS

Prayer is quintessential to the life of every believer, as it is a key component in sustaining the life of the believer. Prayer allows you to build, strengthen, and continuously develop your relationship with God. Prayer permits you to draw close to God. Prayer allows God to endow you with mantles that signify who you are, and what you are assigned to do. Prayer is a limitless arsenal in your journey of faith!

Prayer grants you access to the most holy place. Prayer is the heartbeat of the believer's life. It is as necessary as blood is to the body. Just as inadequate blood flow to body tissues causes discomfort, pain, and death to the affected areas; likewise, an inadequate life of prayer leads to the same both physically and spiritually. It is prayer that keeps you in alignment with the heart and will of God. It is prayer that gives you access and insight to what God has spoken and allowed to be written. When you pray, by faith, you can activate God's word to fully experience and live it.

Why another book about prayer when much has been taught and written about prayer? It is important to know that in each season or dispensation of time, God reveals more. More is revealed, so that we may have greater understanding and insight. The Lord desires for us to intimately connect with His essence through prayer. This allows us to grow deeper and ascend higher in Him. God's word and His inspiration, enlightens and empowers us to comprehend His will and live accordingly.

To live a life pleasing to God, we must know what He desires. To know what He desires, we must know His heart. How do we access the heart of God? We access the heart of God through worship, the study of His word, and through quality time spent in prayer, which is the focus of this writing.

Although prayer is a personal exchange between you and God, prayer must be done from the right perspective, and with the right intent. In other words, "Let all things be done decently and in order" (1 Cor. 14:40). Why? Because there is a structure (arrangement, organization of interrelated elements) that gives prayer its identity, function, strength, and power.

The disciples of Jesus' day witnessed the supernatural manifestations that followed the prayers of Christ. Therefore, they asked to be taught how to pray just as John taught and gave instructions to his disciples on how to pray. The disciples knew how to pray. It was their witness of the greater revelation, purpose, value, and outcome of prayer that caused a deeper desire for even more. When the structures of prayer are properly accessed and utilized, the result is a more effective prayer life. The request of the disciples in Luke 11 verse one, "Lord teach us to pray...," is a great example for us to follow.

Not understanding the various structures and dimensions of prayer causes many to limit prayer to just a time of petitioning (asking). Often, that is done incorrectly. In fact, James 4:3 states: "Ye ask, and receive not, because ye ask amiss (inappropriately, improperly, selfishly, wickedly, & out of alignment) that ye may consume it upon your lusts." The truth of the matter is this: We do not have to ask for what the Lord has already given. Instead, we must learn to access, by faith, what has already been promised. Prayer places you in the right posture to possess what God has for you.

8

Therefore, the mastery of prayer structures is important to the believer. Prayer structures are guides to bring focus and balance to prayer. This leads to a focused and well-balanced life. What you are about to read is not a secret formula designed to get you what you feel you deserve or want. These principles (structures) must always be activated by your faith, through the guidance of the Holy Spirit, to ultimately fulfill what God wants.

For your prayers to be consistent and effective, you must organize and strategically structure your prayers. In James 5:16, it is noted that "the effectual fervent prayer of a righteous man availeth much." This is not solely about praying with passionate emotional energy. It also includes praying on purpose and praying with purpose! To pray without purpose is like going to church without knowing why you are there.

BE PROFICIENT IN PRAYER

Prayer that is effective, heartfelt, and strategic opens heavenly portals that enable natural and spiritual breakthroughs to take place. Mantles fall, spiritual empowerment happens, angelic assistance is obtained, alignment occurs, and ultimately divine enthronement! As the enemy is skilled in his demonic activities, you must be even more skilled in the ministry of spiritual warfare.

You are fighting an unseen enemy that is not moved by physical stature or by vain repetitious words. We are informed in Ephesians 6:12 that "We wrestle not against flesh and blood, but against principalities, against powers, against the rulers of the darkness of this world, against spiritual wickedness in high places."

The kingdom of darkness is well-organized. It is quite competent in its ungodly schemes and plans. Therefore, you must become proficient in prayer. Utilize prayer like a skilled marksman utilizes his weapons of war!

In this book, we will discuss five structures of prayer to instruct and assist you in the growth and development of your prayer life. Strategically arranged prayers enable you to consistently penetrate the heavens to bring God, His kingdom, and His will here to earth. Read this book not just as another book about prayer, but for the purposes of 1) affirming the proper use of prayer, and 2) developing an appreciation of the great value of prayer. Through prayer, we have been granted the awesome privilege of being able to connect and communicate with our Father, in heaven, whenever we choose.

If this book could talk, it would remind you that it is not a secret formula to be used to finally get what you have not been able to get from God. It would tell you that the principles of these structures are to be activated by faith to navigate and penetrate the spiritual realm strategically and successfully. It would tell you prayer is the method to bring earth and all its inhabitants into agreement and divine alignment with all of heaven!

See prayer as a gift to be valued and appreciated. Understand that someone (Jesus) had to die, and be resurrected, for you to have the right to communicate and have unbroken fellowship with God, the Father. This awesome privilege was given not because you deserve it or earned it, but simply because YOU ARE LOVED! Read this book about prayer and be perpetually Blessed!!!

My sincere prayer for you is that you bless other people with the spiritual light within the pages of this book. Simply share this must read with your family, friends, neighbors, and spiritual brothers and sisters. Give them the opportunity to purchase a copy for themselves. Give them the opportunity to enhance their spiritual growth and development. Mark 16:15 states: "And He said unto them, Go ye into all the world, and preach the gospel to every creature."

As you continue reading this book, pray for the blessings that you want to manifest in your life! Take advantage of the valuable information and the personal testimonies shared throughout this book. You now have a direct set of signposts to help guide you along your life's spiritual journey.

– Lawrence Deon Hill

Ephesians 1:18… And [I pray] that the eyes of your heart [the very center and core of your being] may be enlightened [flooded with light by the Holy Spirit], so that you will know and cherish the hope [the divine guarantee, the confident expectation] to which He has called you, the riches of His glorious inheritance in the saints (God's people) (AMP).

STRUCTURAL GUIDE #1

LOCATION:
THE POINT OF FOCUS

Luke 11:2: Our Father which art in heaven, Hallowed be thy name.

CHAPTER ONE

LOCATION: THE POINT OF FOCUS

Two of the most critical times of flight for an airplane are in the takeoff (initial ascent) and in the landing (final approach or descent). In this writing, emphasis is placed on the ascent. When it comes to prayer, how you start can have a direct effect on the outcome. In response to the request of the disciples in the Eleventh Chapter of Luke, the first noted instructions of Christ were that when they pray, they should say: "Our Father which art in heaven, hallowed be thy name."

It is of vital importance that when you begin to pray, you identify who you are speaking to and to where you are directing your prayer. In other words, prayer must have a specific point of focus and a specific location. Our Father identifies who. In heaven indicates the where.

In Psalms 5:2 it states: "Hearken unto the voice of my cry, my King, and my God: for unto thee will I pray." Here the writer makes it clear he is not praying to you, me, ancient ancestors, or any other spirit. He distinctly notes who he is praying to, my King and my God. The writer further states, "My voice shalt thou hear in the morning, O Lord; in the morning will I direct my prayer unto thee and will look up" (Psalms 5:3).

As an example, the writer establishes the importance of directing prayer to the Father (who), and he specifies we are to look up (location). Likewise, when you communicate in prayer to the right person, and you direct your prayer to the right location, the end results are manifested miracles through answered prayers! Prayers in this manner, provide assurance that your prayers will reach their intended destination and result in their intended outcome.

During its journey to its intended destination, a plane in flight may experience turbulence. Turbulence is atmospheric instability that results in violent unsteady movement of the air. This causes a shaking or sudden and unplanned drop in altitude of the plane requiring adjustments for stabilization. The plane may also experience drag. Drag is the force that opposes the plane's movement through the air. Its effect causes a delay or slowing down of the plane's forward progression.

Similarly, prayers may also experience turbulence or drag, if not communicated to the right person in the right location. In addition to the right person and the right location, prayers should also include the use of strategic language. It is often said, it is not what you say when you pray; it is how you say it. Many believe that God knows the heart and understands the language of tears.

There is some truth to that. However, the complete truth is that it indeed matters what you say, how you say it, and to whom you say it.

Understand that words have power, for they are spirit and life. Your prayers take flight by your words. Not understanding the power of words, coupled with inadequate or improper use of language, leads to praying amiss. Praying inappropriately, with the wrong intent, or with dishonor may lead to the releasing of words that may cancel your requests or petitions. It may also cause a delay or hindrance to your spiritual growth and progression in prayer.

How you approach God, and the language you use, reveal the content of your heart. It, too, reveals your attitude about God. Most importantly, it indicates your relationship or lack thereof with God. What you say and how you say it becomes important because it flows from the heart. King David said, "Let the words of my mouth, and the meditation of my heart, be acceptable in thy sight, O Lord, my strength, and my redeemer" (Psalms 19:14). It is important that your words be properly aligned with God's heart.

Over the years, it has been incorrectly taught and still accepted as a truth that when you pray, just pray from your heart. Well, that sounds good, but it is not entirely true. The heart cannot be trusted. How do we know this? It is written in Jeremiah 17:9 that "the heart is deceitful above all things, and desperately wicked: who can know it?" Additionally, Matthew 15:19 tells us "For out of the heart proceed evil thoughts, murders, adulteries, fornications, thefts, false witness, and blasphemies."

This lets us know that it is dangerous to just pray from the heart alone. We must also pray in and with the Holy Spirit. This does not necessarily mean you pray in tongues. It means that you are to submit to the guidance of the Holy Spirit. Allow Him to lead you.

17

You do not lead Him. This important point will be discussed in detail later in this writing.

In truth, we do not really know how or even know what we should pray about. Romans 8:26 states it is the Holy Spirit that helps our limitations and intercedes for us with groanings that we could not express with our limited and finite words. We need the aid of the Holy Spirit because He is the revealer of truth. It is He who knows and searches all things. He knows the content of our hearts and the motives of why we pray.

PRAYER AIDED BY THE HOLY SPIRIT

Understand also that praying in the Holy Spirit is what gives our prayers distinction from those who are not in covenant relationship with God, through Jesus. Mankind, without the assistance of the Holy Spirit, will not be able to discern or receive the things of God. This is so, because the mind and will, of the unconverted individual, rejects the things of God.

Praying in the Holy Spirit enables you to know, speak, and live out the things of God. Additionally, the Holy Spirit empowers you to pray with purpose and precision. It allows God to put His words in your mouth and not your words in His mouth. Praying from the heart alone does not allow the Holy Spirit to divinely align your heart with what God wants. Prayer directed by the Holy Spirit deals with the spirit of the heart, relieving the natural weaknesses of the heart.

Therefore, mastery of meditation is important. It is a valuable part of your prayer life. Meditation helps to focus your mind. It helps to shut out distractions. It prepares and positions you, so the Holy Spirit can pray through your heart, and not just out of your heart. Meditation also assists you to think reflectively. It helps bring you into position to gain insight into the deeper revelations.

Joshua 1:8 states: "This book of the law (God's word) shall not depart out of thy mouth; but thou shalt meditate (think, ponder, and muse over) therein day and night, that thou mayest observe to do according to all that is written therein: for then thou shalt make thy way prosperous, and then thou shalt have good success."

In other words, never allow the revelation of God's word to be out of your heart, mind, or daily practices. This enables your lifestyle to consistently lead you to victory and prosperity. A good structure for meditation before you pray includes reading the word of God. Meditate on the word of God, then pray by the Spirit of God.

Structuring prayer is important, because petitions made with right words but the wrong heart, or the right heart with the wrong words, limit God in His response. It may also lead to unanswered petitions. Consider, however, what happens when a right heart, matured in prayer, is coupled with strategic language. The result is a more effective prayer life. This will be evidenced by divine encounters and supernatural manifestations.

Let us further examine why it is important to identify who we are praying to, and why our focus must be solely on God. Recall Christ's instructions to His disciples in Luke 11:2: "When ye pray, say: Father, hallowed be thy name" (NIV). These instructions let us know that we cannot pray without mentioning and greatly reverencing the name of our Lord. Calling His name gets His attention, in the same manner, as when we call the name of our spouse or child. They respond and no one else. Should someone else inadvertently respond, you make sure to clarify to whom you were speaking.

Specifically calling His name ensures that the true and living God will respond and not some other spirit source. Failing to hallow or honor His name may cause a delay in receiving His response. Know that when you hallow His name, you draw His glory. When you draw His glory, you draw His power. To hallow His name means to set His name apart, honor His name as holy, and to esteem it higher than any other name. In hallowing His name, you acknowledge the sanctity and sacredness of His name.

When you hallow His name, you recognize the power and authority of His name. Because of this, you are mindful to not reduce His name to a thing of commonality. When you regard His name as holy, you do not use His name in vain. You do not call on Him as you would call your friend or next-door neighbor.

The emphasis of hallowing the name of the Lord is made because what we say and how we address our Lord, in prayer, reveals your heart towards Him. It also reveals the depth of your relationship with Him. When you have a true love for God, it should be difficult to use His name in vain. It should be uncomfortable to call Him by anything other than His holy name. So, before you bring your petitions to the Heavenly Father, you must first bring your praise. You must first magnify and glorify God, the Father. You must make God big!

MAKE GOD BIG!!!

Making God big means you cause Him to become larger and greater than your problems. When you enlarge God over your situations and circumstances, you cause your heart, mind, and will, to come into the very center and core of His presence. You become focused. Your flow in prayer then becomes easier. Ultimately, you ascend to an altitude in prayer where it is no longer a struggle to pray.

Often, we do not pray, or we are ineffective in prayer, because our hearts and words are fixed on the problem, or on our own limitations. We make the problems bigger than what they should be. We often stay in situations longer than we need to. Our focus is on the issue instead of on our God who has the solutions to all problems.

Colossians 3:2 states: "Set your affection on things above, not on things on the earth." Your current trouble is just the turbulence and drag that the enemy uses to delay and deny you of what is rightfully yours. God uses it to mature and propel you into the fulfillment of your destiny and purpose. Enlarge God by hallowing His name. Hallowing His name means you acknowledge His providence, splendor, beauty, and His ability to do and become whatever you need when you need it.

When you enlarge God through the hallowing of His name, complaints are replaced with praise. It allows you to give your cares to the Lord and align your heart with His. This allows Him and His will to become the sole focus of your communication and fellowship with Him. Then watch as your temporary problems become insignificant in the presence of the eternal and Sovereign God!

As you read throughout this book, you will notice that some words referring to God, the Father; Christ, the Son; or the Holy Spirt will be capitalized. This is not necessarily grammatically correct. However, it is done with purpose as an example of hallowing or setting apart the triune Godhead. This shows high regard and honor for His name even in the writing of this book.

His name reflects His Majesty, Sovereignty, Holiness, and His glory! His name reflects His goodness, His mercy and grace, His ability to forgive, deliver, set free, and so much more! We also know that the name of our Lord is powerful as stated in Philippians 2:9-10 (AMP): "...God has highly exalted Him and freely bestowed on Him the name, which is above every name, so that at the name of Jesus every knee shall bow (in submission) of those who are in heaven and on earth and under the earth..."

So, before you declare your list of petitions, hallow the name of the Lord. Call upon Him in truth. Then build a place of defense (a place of shelter, provision, protection, and strength) with His Holy name. Hide in His name. Why? "The name of the Lord is a strong tower: the righteous runneth into it and is safe" (Prov. 18:10).

Reverence His holy name and draw both His Presence and His righteous kingdom into your sphere. Esteem high His name and be drawn near to His throne. Hallowing His name enables you to be in your assigned place. It ensures you are in the right posture to encounter the Holy King. It positions you to fully access what is rightfully yours!

The words of prayer are like seeds. For a seed to produce a harvest, it must be planted in the right soil at the right time.

Likewise, with prayer, it must be directed to the right person and the right place. Our hearts and minds must be focused on who we are praying to, and what we are praying about. This distinction of hallowing the name of the Lord is noted here because in ancient times, they believed in polytheism (more than one god). For example, if rain were needed, a prayer would be made to the rain god. If fertility were the need, the prayer would be directed to the god of fertility. This distinction is also made to impress upon you the significance of ensuring that when you pray, your prayers have focus, direction, intent, and purpose.

Do not be like the Pharisees', of biblical times, who prayed to be seen and heard using empty words and vain repetitions. Their hearts and minds were focused on self. Their words were directed to the people who heard them versus the God who could answer them. Their intent and purpose were for their own personal glory, and not the glory of God. The principle of directing your prayers is in alignment with what God, our Creator, did in the beginning. When He spoke to various aspects of the firmament and the earth, He gave His words a focal point and a destiny. That then gave to us what we now know as heaven and earth.

Isaiah 55:11 tells us clearly that the words of God will not come back to Him unfulfilled. They will accomplish and perform the purpose for which He spoke them. Prayers are prophetic decrees according to the word and will of God. Therefore, when you pray, shut out everything else. Pray the scriptures, and give back to the living God, in heaven, what He has already said. Then watch the Creator, source, and sustainer of all things, honor His words to achieve your requests.

In addition to directing prayer to the right person, you must also direct them to the right place. Location is also vital to communication. Through prayer, you can shorten the distance between you and God. Remember, Jesus said to His disciples that when praying they are to say, "Our Father, which art in heaven." Directing your prayers to the specific location of heaven, where our heavenly Father rules and reigns from, ensures that He who can answer and fulfill all requests will do so.

Jesus demonstrated this principle in the feeding of the multitude with two fish and five loaves (Luke 9:16-17). This miracle occurred after Jesus looked up to heaven (location) and gave thanks to God (source). This act of directing prayer to the right person and the right location resulted in thousands of people being fed to the point of being satisfied. In the end, twelve baskets of broken pieces were gathered.

Manifestations of supernatural results like this example can be a part of your daily bread. Ensure that your prayers are directed to the right source, the right location, and are in alignment with His plans and purposes. Jeremiah 29:11 (NIV) tells us: "For I know the plans I have for you, declares the Lord, plans to prosper you and not to harm you, plans to give you hope and a future."

By faith, we can access those plans and bring them here into our present time. His plans can propel us into our future. For many, this is not a reality. Instead of praying to the heavenly Father and giving praise as Christ did, there is often much complaining. Complaints give life to the problem. It does not allow you to access heaven or bring forth the plans and purposes of the Lord.

Christ both taught and demonstrated this principle of praying to the right source and the right location. He understood that both were vital in laying the foundation for answered prayers with supernatural results. He knew that for the disciples then, and us today, to call into existence what does not exist, and to speak life to what is dying or dead, we must know where to go and who to ask.

You cannot go to the office store and ask for a specific type of hamburger or sandwich. You could, but you would not get what you were hoping for. The point is this, it is critical how you start and end prayer! Therefore, when you pray, your heart and mind must be set on bringing what is in heaven here to be established in the earth. That will not be sufficiently done if your prayers are not directed to the right person and sent to the right place.

The link between the right person and place is about communication. It is communication that brings people and places together. Many of life's issues are, in part, due to a breakdown of communication. It may be a lack of communication or miscommunication. Communication involves a minimum of two parties. One must clearly convey the intended message. The other must accurately receive what was clearly conveyed.

When the intended system of communication collapses or fails, frustration and delay are the end results. It is imperative to ensure that your prayers are directed to the right person and the right place, as they are interdependent. To misroute your prayer is like making a telephone call and dialing the wrong number or getting a number that is disconnected. It is also like sending a letter with the wrong name or an incomplete or incorrect address. It will be returned to the sender and marked as undeliverable.

Similarly, the results of a misguided prayer mean the requests, needs, and cries for help and intervention are not received. There will be no response because the prayer never reached the intended person or location. I place great emphasis on praying to the right person, in the right location, and utilizing strategic language with the help of the Holy Spirit. Why? Because it is God alone who has eyes to see, ears to hear, as well as the authority and power to respond timely and strategically!

Understand also that when prayer is released, the expectation must always be for an eternal response. For that reason, when you pray, do not be concerned about time. To do so, prevents you from getting through the layers of prayer. Time is a stoppage in eternity that affects and restricts mankind. It does not limit our God who transcends time and is able to redeem time. You cannot operate in eternity with a time zone mentality. You must stop putting God in your time zone and allow space, in time, for eternity. Eternity cannot invade time when you remain in control through time. So, stop giving God time, and give Him space!

GIVE GOD TIME AND SPACE!

Do not just give God time, give Him space. What does that really mean? It means, do not try to control the conversation based on the time you have, or what you feel you want to give. You are only in control of time in that you function in time. In prayer, there should be ascension. For that to happen, you must step out of time and into eternity when you pray. Seek to transition out of time and into eternal space, God's space. Space, in this instance, means unlimited measure. Do not seek to restrict or control God. This is what often happens within our minds.

We limit God because we remain in time. Time is what constrains the thoughts and actions of man, but not God. Become aware that when you enter communion and communication with the righteous and Holy God, you cannot enter in and try to put Him on your time schedule. Do not, I repeat, do not try to dictate how the conversation goes. Even if all you have is ten minutes, in those ten minutes, give God full control!

God does not want you to disregard the time you have, because you live and operate in time. Understand that He must have control because He is Sovereign and eternal. Therefore, remove the limits. God can give you more in ten minutes than you can get on your own, in your entire lifetime. He can do this because His thoughts are not your thoughts, neither are your ways His ways (Isaiah 55:8). It is God who controls time from His eternity. Eternity is where all things are to be given back to Him. Every time you step into God's eternal space, God fine-tunes and perfects all that you give to Him.

It is just like when you take your car to the dealer for a tune-up. They go through the car's systems upgrading and restoring what has been worn by the wear and tear of time. Allow God's eternal wisdom to restore and realign all aspects of your life effected by the wear and tear of time. Prayer is where you let go of your beginning and your end to allow God the space to do in your time what you cannot.

I conclude this section with this: when possible, be mindful to try and set an atmosphere that is favorable for Jesus, the King. Start by giving your undivided attention. It is disheartening to try and have an intimate conversation with someone who is preoccupied with something or someone else. Begin with a quiet undisturbed place. Read the word and listen to songs of praise and worship to help bring your heart and mind into focus. You may then choose to switch to instrumental music and sing your own Spirit-given songs to the Lord. He indeed longs to hear directly from you.

Allow the wind of the Holy Spirit to carry your words to the throne room of God. Love on God with words of adoration and appreciation. Seek guidance, ask for wisdom and strength, and intercede for others as Christ, the Savior, intercedes for you. Make your requests, then expect to receive and experience tangible revelations and manifestations of God's unfailing promises. Your divinely aligned prayers will pull all of heaven into your sphere!

Lastly, remember to enter the presence of the Holy King with a heart of humility. Spend time surrendering yourself to the Almighty God before you begin making your requests. When entering the presence of authority, ancient customs required individuals to bow before speaking. Likewise, remember to not only bow your knees, but fully submit your mind, heart, and will to the Sovereignty of God.

This is a good place to apply what you have read thus far. Before continuing to read, pause here and hallow the name of the Holy King. Here is an example for you to follow.

PRAYER

My God and Holy King, I lift my head, my heart, and my soul unto you. O God of heaven, you are Jehovah, the God that becomes whatever I need when I am in need. I acknowledge your Sovereignty and in humble submission, I give myself to you. Hear now your servant's prayer as I posture myself at the feet of your throne. I am grateful that your love is unfailing and that your majesty is better than life. Therefore, I will forever honor you. With the fruit of my lips, I will sing praises to your Holy and Righteous name forever, amen!

– Lawrence Deon Hill

CALL TO ACTION...consider the prayer guide you just read. Meditate on the example prayer, then write your own personal prayer.

STRUCTURAL GUIDE #2

TRANSITIONAL SHIFTING:

WHAT HEAVEN WANTS

Luke 11:2: Thy Kingdom come. Thy will be done, as in heaven, so in earth...

CHAPTER TWO

TRANSITIONAL SHIFTING: WHAT HEAVEN WANTS

I can remember this day as if it were yesterday because it was an experience that greatly challenged my faith as a believer. The day was a beautiful, sunny day. The entire family was joyous, and the wife and I had fallen in love all over again! It was the day we were moving into our first home. Everything was perfect; so, I thought. My wife and children were outside loading things in the car. I was in the house, upstairs in the bathroom, collecting other items to be moved. Suddenly, I heard the screech of tires and then the impact of a car hitting something.

The next sound I heard was the voice of people screaming, but the voice that was clear to me, was that of my wife. I ran down the stairs and outside to see my wife holding our youngest daughter who was about 2 years old at the time. I saw the blood around her mouth. Without thinking, I grabbed our daughter from my wife and ran back upstairs into the bathroom. As she was screaming, I held her in my arms. I rocked her. As I was cleaning her face, I went into prayer!

I prayed against broken bones and internal injuries. I called forth the healing virtue of the Lord! I declared healing is the children's bread. I invoked the power of Jehovah Raphe, the Lord our Healer. Although I heard the ambulance coming, it was not until someone came to get me that I brought her down to be examined by the paramedics.

As they checked and inspected her small flailing body from head to toe, I continued to pray. The only thing they found was that one of her front teeth had been knocked backward by the impact of the car. They recommended she be taken to the hospital. In fact, everyone wanted me to take her to the hospital, but I said, "no!" I announced to everyone present that she was fine, and we were going to continue our move!

I was not about to let our perfect day be ruined! The family was angry, my wife was apprehensive, and I was fighting my own inner annoyance with the whole situation. My baby had gotten hit by a car, her tooth was displaced, and not everyone was happy with my decision. All I had was my faith. In that, I called for her healing to manifest in the earth (in her body) as it was already done in heaven.

The next day, I got a call from my mother who emphatically shared her displeasure with my decision. Then, I received a call from my father, who stated he understood my stance of faith, but he, too, insisted that I should have taken her to the hospital, so they could confirm my faith that she was alright. After that call, my inner man was broken and crushed. I went into the bathroom, got on my knees, and cried out to God. My face was soaked with tears as I said, "Lord, I believe you, and I believe your word. Did I do the right thing?" As I cried out in anguish, the Lord spoke to me and said, "Son, stand your ground!"

OBJECT OF GOD'S OBJECTIVES

I felt reassured by the word of the Lord. I dried my tears and released that burden of doubt and fear. Two days later, my daughter's tooth had returned to its right position. My faith and prayers became the objects by which God's objective of healing could transition from the spirit to be seen in the natural.

That was an example of transitional shifting! What is transitional shifting? What does it mean to become the object of God's objectives? Transitional shifting is the change or movement of something from one place to another. More specifically, shifting from heaven to earth or from the spirit to the natural. This is important as the embodiment of prayer is to get what heaven has. As we pray, we must have the mind to shift all of heaven's functions and operations to earth.

We must pray with the understanding that the central and most important part of prayer is to pray for what God wants (His will and His desires). Recall Luke 11:2: "Thy kingdom come. Thy will be done, as in heaven, so in earth...". This essential portion of prayer allows the earth to mirror heaven. It allows your life here to reflect what He already said & did there, in heaven. In other words, whatever happens in heaven should also happen here in the earth. The same principles in operation there, should be in operation here.

Before continuing, let us briefly define two concepts that I believe are key to the principle of transitional shifting. They are language and communication. Language is defined as the system or method of communication used and understood by different groups of people to express thoughts, ideas, and feelings. Communication is the process in which words and sounds are used to express or exchange information.

Communication allows people and places to connect. It does not matter if your native language is grammatically correct or a broken dialect. What really matters is that you know the heart of God. How do you come to know God's heart? You must know and understand His word which is comprised of His will, intents, passions, and desires.

Knowing His word allows you to know what He loves and what He despises. You know what He accepts and what He rejects. The most effective way to communicate with God and bring heaven to earth is to pray the word of God. God's written word reveals what He has already spoken. When you speak what God has said, it becomes a living word to fulfill its purpose.

Recall the story of creation in which we read how God created the heavens and the earth. Every time God said let there be, whatever He spoke to produced what He said. God said let there be light and there was light. God said let the waters under the heaven be gathered unto one place and let dry land appear, and it happened. It was God's will for what was unseen to become seen. Therefore, He spoke, and the invisible appeared in a visible form.

By His word, God's creative power caused something to come from nothing. God never calls anything into existence without a reason or specific purpose in mind. With that in mind, understand the core function of transitional shifting. It is the process by which what is in heaven is communicated to tangibly manifest in the earth. We are the principal objects by which God's objectives become known. He communicates to and through us.

At the time of my daughter's injury, instead of focusing on the events of the accident, the word of the Lord came to me concerning healing. As I declared His word by faith, my prayer brought forth God's healing virtue from the spirit into the natural. We are co-creators in the earth, just as God is the Creator in heaven. How do we know this? Genesis 1:26 tells us we were created in His image and after His likeness. He is Elohim the Creator and Sustainer of all the earth. In fact, Hebrews 1:3 informs us that He upholds all things by the word of His power.

By His spoken word, all things are affirmed, confirmed, maintained, and supported. As co-creators, we have both the privilege and the responsibility to bring all of heaven to earth. The creative functions of prayer enable us to operate as God did in creation. Prayer allows us to see the unseen and call it into existence. Speak His word according to His will. At the appointed hour, what you have spoken will come to pass, because God honors (fulfills) His word!

This is revelation that your adversary does not want you to know or competently operate in. With knowledge and understanding of this insight, you must no longer live life with the mindset, "it is what it is." Know that you can cause life's situations to come into alignment with what God has already said. All you need to do is declare His word, according to His will.

What is God's will in relation to your circumstances? Have you earnestly called for His eternal kingdom to come and bring alignment to your life on earth? Do you speak how you feel, or do you speak what you seek? Do you say what you see, or do you say what God has said? Do you declare God's glory, or do you suffer in silence? When you speak what God has already spoken, you invoke His authoritative power to work on your behalf.

What are you speaking? Do you routinely speak about your problems? Do you dwell on how they frustrate you, and how things never seem to change? Do you complain more than you pray? Or are you one who will seek to know what God says about the problem and you pray that? If you are the latter, you are more likely to see tangible manifestations of God's kingdom in your life.

Kingdom encounters in the earth should not be random, unexpected occurrences. They should be a part of your daily existence. Especially, if you are a believer. Why then is this not routinely so? Why does it often seem believers are more in awe when miracles occur than seemingly non-believers? There are many reasons for this and many factors that influence those reasons. For the purposes of this reading, I submit to you the following three interrelated reasons: 1) God's will is not the object of our affections, 2) we are not consistently available to become the object of God's objectives, and 3) we do not consistently say or pray what God has already said.

First, God's will is not consistently the object of our affections. Colossians 3:2 admonishes that we are to set our affection on things above, not on things on the earth. The things that we are attracted to should be that which is spiritual and eternal instead of that which is natural and temporary. This is important to transitional shifting. If your mind is solely tied to what is in the earth, you cannot pull from heaven. If your focus is only on what you want, you cannot know what heaven wants.

KNOW WHAT HEAVEN WANTS

Make God and His kingdom the object of your affections. Then, you will not have to try and figure out how to get what you need or want. By His Spirit, He will direct you. He will open the windows of heaven and pour out His blessings upon you (Malachi 3:10). Understand that God will never place your personal wishes above His divine will. In truth, you should not want anything above His will. As stated before, you must desire and long for what God wants. The will of God becomes the object of your affections when you delight yourself in Him.

A common error made by many is they want the blessings of the kingdom, but not the King or His governance. Therefore, much time is spent petitioning when transitioning should be taking place. Pray for the revelation and the manifestation of the King, and the blessings of the kingdom will follow. This is pointed out for us in Matthew 6:33: "But seek ye first the kingdom of God, and His righteousness; and all these things shall be added unto you." In addition, grasp the truth of 2 Peter 1:3: "According as His divine power hath given unto us all things that pertain unto life and godliness…".

You already have whatever you need when you need it. Through prayer, now is the time to access it by faith. Cause it to move or shift from heaven and come to where the need is. Your prayer life should not be influenced by your conditions. Your conditions should be influenced or changed by your prayers! Please, understand that prayers are not just mere words. Words of prayer are spirit and life. Through prayer, you can bring forth the abundant life provided in the Savior, Jesus, the Christ!

Secondly, we do not regularly make ourselves available to become the object by which God's objectives can be released into the earth. I emphasize that God wants the unseen to become seen. God wants what He has spoken in heaven to be made tangible and received in the earth. He wants His promises to transition from spoken and written words to lived experiences. For it to be so, He needs a conduit or object. When God wanted all of creation to know Him, He sent His Son from heaven to earth in a natural body.

The unseen deity became seen. This allowed Jesus to make known on earth the heart, character, and will of the Father. When the disciples saw Jesus, they saw the Father. When they heard the teachings of Jesus, they heard the wisdom of the Father. The love Jesus showed them was the love of the Father. The ministry of Jesus consistently brought heaven to earth. Everything Jesus did and said pointed to the Father, in Heaven. As a result of Christ's transitional works, reconciliation and restoration can continue to manifest through our prayers.

When you present your body as a living sacrifice, you fully surrender your heart and will to Him. You become the conduit by which all of heaven is reflected in the earth. You become the vessel or object by which the objectives of God and His kingdom are made known. When others see you, they should see God and His glory. When others hear you speak, they should hear the voice and words of God. They should come to know the heart of God. The King and His Kingdom is made known when you sincerely want what heaven wants.

Once you know what heaven wants, then decree, declare, proclaim, and prophesy it! Pray for God's kingdom to come and His will to be done. You have the privilege to become the object of God's objectives. You have the authority to use inanimate objects like God did. You can also speak to objects just like Jesus did.

When there is a need for the manifestation of the kingdom, God can and will use objects to manifest His glory. For example, the rod of Moses was turned into a snake then back to a rod. This was validation of the authenticity of Moses' mission before the elders of Israel. The rod was also used to demonstrate God's Sovereign power and authority over the pagan gods of Egypt. In Mark 11:14, Jesus speaks to the fig tree, and it obeyed Him when it withered and died.

In Matthew 8:26-27, Jesus rebuked the wind and the sea bringing about a great calm. The disciples were in awe of Him as a man demonstrating that kind of power. Being led by the Holy Spirit, we can also pray and utilize objects to carry out the will of God. Understand, however, that it is not about man showing his power.

It is about manifesting God's glory and shifting what has already been done, in heaven, to now be done in the earth. The heavens declare God's glory and speak of His existence, sovereignty, and dominion. In like manner, the things we do and possess in the earth should tell of His goodness and not ours. We must be mindful not to commit the error of reverencing people and their gifts. We must also be sure to always give honor and reverence to God as the giver of the gifts. It is through transitional shifting that we make Jesus and His righteous kingdom known.

Third, we do not consistently, by faith, proclaim what God has already said. In many instances, this is because we do not know what He has said. Or we do not believe what God has said. It is difficult to believe what you do not know. What you do not know, you will not trust. What you do not trust, may cause doubt and disbelief until there is something seen or proven.

Thomas, one of the apostles, was informally given the nickname doubting Thomas. His skepticism caused him to require proof that Jesus had indeed resurrected (see St. John, Chapter 20). Thomas refused to believe or accept that Jesus had resurrected and appeared to the other apostles. Until he could have the opportunity to see and feel the wounds of Jesus, he stated, he would not believe.

We may not admit it, but at times we feel like Thomas. Our actions show evidence of disbelief when we do not consistently activate what we say we know and believe. Belief should always produce action. You will do or say something to indicate that you indeed believe. To believe takes faith. We read it throughout the scriptures that wherever there was faith, it produced an action. The action led to manifestation.

The consistent manifestation of what God promised is often not seen. In many instances, the word of God is reduced to mere clichés and common sayings. These are recited in attempts to sound spiritual or appear intellectually deep. Quoting scripture without understanding, and without proper application, makes it difficult to get what heaven has.

PRAYING GOD'S WORD

It is imperative that we understand the purpose and power of praying God's word. This must be a part of our everyday lives. It is not just for a show during church programs or other religious gatherings. Do you really know God's word? Do you fully believe His word? I encourage you to believe His word, trust His word, and have faith in His word. Do not be like those who simply hope the word is true and believe only after the word has come to pass. Jesus said to Thomas, "…blessed are they that have not seen, and yet have believed" (St. John 20:29).

Transitional shifting is about bringing the kingdom of heaven, and the will of God into the earth to make seen the unseen. Consider the following two questions: Is the kingdom physical or spiritual? Is it a present kingdom or future kingdom? Although there is some tangibility to the kingdom, the essence of the kingdom is not physical. When Jesus came into the earth to reveal himself as King, this was an issue for Israel.

They were looking for an Israelite King, to overthrow the Roman Empire, and liberate them from the oppression of Rome. Even at that time, Jesus did not declare a physical kingdom. Instead, He repeatedly taught and demonstrated that His kingdom was not of this world. In the 14th Chapter of St. John, He lets us know that there is a tangible place of existence in the heavenlies. Jesus stated, He was going away to prepare a place and that He would come back to receive His own, unto Himself.

In other words, there is a perceivable and discernable place that God is preparing. That prepared place is for those who are His.

43

This lets us know that the kingdom is both spiritual and tangible. Lay hold of this truth: The kingdom is wherever God is. Wherever God's presence and power is revealed, in that, is the manifestation of the kingdom.

When you think of the kingdom, do not limit it to what is known or experienced by the natural senses alone. Romans 14:17 tells us: "For the kingdom of God is not meat and drink but righteousness, and peace, and joy in the Holy Ghost." Do not limit the kingdom to any one identifiable place nor one specific type of people. Instead, allow your faith to cause what is in heaven to come to the earth. Through faith, God's authority, and power manifests. In that, is the evidence that the kingdom is present, productive, and in operation.

The kingdom is everywhere because Jesus said the kingdom is within us. When we limit the kingdom to a tangible place, we miss the vastness of God and His kingdom. The vastness of the kingdom is uncontainable, just like God. We reveal the kingdom when we establish places for God to manifest His presence and perform His will. We advance the kingdom when we show the reign of our God through our righteous works. We expand the kingdom when the life of God is produced more abundantly, through us, wherever we go.

It is of necessity that we pray for Sovereign God to manifest His kingdom in and through us. The life of God is not meant to stay within us. It is to flow out of us like rivers of living waters. It is noted in St. John 7:38: "...out of his (your) belly shall flow rivers of living water." Through willing and intentional acts of obedience, the kingdom flows and manifests. In this season, we need the visible governance of God's righteous kingdom.

Why do we need God's governance? Man has not sufficiently shown that he can govern himself. In Genesis 1:26, we read how God created man in His image and likeness. He blessed him and gave instructions to multiply and replenish the earth. He then gave dominion over all the earth. It is humanity's responsibility to work and watch over God's earthly creations!

Unfortunately, man has used his dominion to control and rule over people. This has led to repeated cycles of division, hatred, suffering, violence, and death. The way to end these destructive cycles and usher in the principles of love, forgiveness, unity, and peace is through God's kingdom. Know that it pleases God to give access to His kingdom (Luke 12:32).

When you pray, ensure that your prayers are enveloped and sealed by the Holy name of Jesus. This assures that your prayers reach the Heavenly Father for His response. It is noted in St. John 16:23 that if we ask anything (according to His will) in the name of Jesus, the Father will give it. Then will you see heaven's provisions manifest. Then you will experience the coming of His kingdom, and the fulfillment of His will. That is transitional shifting!

Before continuing, think of a current stressor or pressing problem in your life. Honestly evaluate it to see where the reality of that issue is not reflecting God's truth. Then apply this principle to shift it from what it is to what heaven wants and has just for you!

PRAYER

Eternal God, you called me forth from my mother's womb. You sculpted me in formation as a beautiful picture of your love. You have given me power and authority to speak on your behalf, and for that I praise you. Therefore, I will proclaim your word here in the earth as it was proclaimed already in heaven. By faith, I believe what you want shall come to pass; heavenly vibrations manifesting eternal structures that mirrors heaven. So again, I say, what you want shall come to pass in Jesus name, amen!

– Lawrence Deon Hill

CALL TO ACTION...consider the prayer guide you just read. Meditate on the example prayer. Now, write your own personal prayer.

STRUCTURAL GUIDE #3

DAILY SUFFICIENCY:

YOUR DAILY BREAD

Luke 11:3: Give us day by day our daily bread...

CHAPTER THREE

DAILY SUFFICIENCY: YOUR DAILY BREAD

"Give us day by day our daily bread" (Luke 11:3). This portion of the prayer is easy for most to pray because it involves asking for daily needs. In its simplicity, daily sufficiency means what is sufficient for the day. However, please consider for a moment the following event.

In the 16th Chapter of Exodus, we read about the children of Israel after their deliverance from Egypt, and they find themselves in the wilderness. Being hungry, they complained to Moses and Aaron. Unappreciative of their divine deliverance, they stated they wished they had died in Egypt. It was there that provisions were seemingly more readily available. In truth, they were enslaved under the rule of a hard taskmaster.

In response to their complaint, God sent quails and manna (meat and bread). They were instructed to take only the amount of manna sufficient for the day and were not to leave any until the morning. However, there were those who disregarded the instructions and gathered more. By morning, the extra manna "bred worms and stank" (v. 20). That was indicative of distrust in the same God that had supernaturally rescued them from their enslavement in Egypt.

Consider the following parable told by Jesus in Luke 12:16-21. In this parable, Jesus admonishes against the sin of covetousness. In this example, the land of the rich man produced so much that he said within his own heart that he would tear down his current barns and build greater ones to store his possessions. Possessions that would satisfy him for years. All he needed to do was relax, eat, drink, and enjoy his abundance. It was in that moment that God said to him, "Thou fool, this night thy soul shall be required of thee: then whose shall those things be, which thou hast provided?" (v. 20).

In verse 21, Jesus makes His point. The rich man's security in his personal wealth was indicative of his trust in his own abilities and accomplishments. There was no regard or honor for God. Too often, the desire for more and the desire for wealth reveal a lack of trust in God's ability to meet your needs. If not careful, this lack of trust can lead to self-reliance, self-indulgence, and failure to honor God. Know that there is more to life than the acquirement of material possessions. Keep that in mind as you read to understand the principle of daily sufficiency.

It is often presumed that sufficiency only means enough. In truth, there is abundance in the daily provisions of God. In fact, sufficiency not only means having that which is needful; more importantly, it means having enough and some leftover. God gives what is sufficient for you. Even in that, there is some leftover. The issue is, often the seed to be sown, and the bread to be eaten, are all consumed upon the desires of the individual. This leaves nothing for the individual or anyone else.

Recall the story of the two fish and five loaves. When viewed from the natural or intellectual perspective only, all you see is what is provided for the day. You do not see that within the two fish and five loaves there is enough for now and more for later. The abundance was in the sufficiency.

It is God who puts the abundance in what is sufficient for the day. However, if motives are not right, and if there is no intent to honor God, then the abundance, within what is sufficient, will never be seen. You will then find yourself toiling for more when the more is already in what you currently have. The abundance of your daily provisions is seen when the intent of the heart is to honor the Heavenly Father, and to do His will.

Jesus knew when he told them to feed the company of people that there were only two fish and five loaves. He knew the boy only had what was seemingly sufficient for him. Jesus also knew that more could come out of it by first honoring the Father. By this, Jesus was establishing a life principle for us to follow.

When we honor God with what is sufficient for the day, He then opens our eyes to see the abundance inside of what we have. We would not and could not see it on our own. We often lack the faith or confidence to believe and trust Him. Just as Israel did in the wilderness or like the rich man concerning his personal wealth. Additionally, understand that in this principle of daily sufficiency, you are to pray for what you can manage. The second portion of Proverbs 30:8 states: "...give me neither poverty nor riches; feed me with food convenient for me."

In other words, give me my daily bread or what is sufficient for me. Verse 9 explains why. If too much is given, it may lead to independence (self-sufficiency) and denial of the need for God (like the rich man). If too little is given, then it may lead to stealing or other forms of ill-gotten gains and cause dishonor unto God. Pray for what God has appointed for you to have. Pray for what God has divinely purposed for you to be and do. Your abundance is in your purpose.

Abundance is in God's purpose for all things, as He continues to call things out of things as He did in creation. In the earth realm, all things have something within it that is needed by some other part of creation. Within you, there is something that someone else or some part of creation needs. Therefore, want what God wants you to have, not what you want to have.

Delight yourself in Him and want what He wants and has for you. When you align yourself with what God has for you, your desires will be born out of His will. Simply put, God's will is what He wants for you, not what He wants from you. Pause and consider that for a moment.

GOD GIVES MORE THAN WHAT HE ASKS FOR

When you give yourself to God, He calls for those things that are needed from you. It becomes easy to give yourself to God when you understand what He wants for you. As previously stated, what He wants FOR you, is far greater than what He wants FROM you. The tithe is one source of proof regarding that truth. He only asks for 10% and wants you to have the remaining 90%. He wants to give you more than He wants from you.

God will never ask for more than He is willing and wanting to give you. What the righteous king wants for the people is always greater. He gives more to the people causing them to rejoice. On the other hand, when the wicked are in authority, the people are distressed. Wicked rulers extract more from the people than they are willing to give.

When it comes to daily sufficiency, you need not worry about what or how much God gives. Trust that every portion He gives you, in the various stages of life, is what you can manage during that season. However, know that God has so much more for you! Do not look at what you have or do not have. Instead, set your sights and affections on the Almighty God to see and acquire what He has for you.

Do not focus on what is or is not. Focusing on the now often leads to deceptive behaviors, because you feel like you do not have enough. You feel like you must obtain it now rather than later. As a result, you do not honor God with what you already have. As well, much time is spent dwelling on what is missing and devising schemes to get it.

Having a poverty mentality causes you to steal or obtain positions and possessions without legal rights. This is done because, in truth, you really do not know what He wants for you. You ask for more, before you are grateful for what is sufficient. You ask for more than you have the capacity to handle. When you have too much, the tendency is to act as if you gave it to yourself. Recall the parable of the rich man and his goods.

God reminded Israel then, and reminds you today, you are not to forget your God who provides and protects. You are not to think or say your success is the result of your own power or might. It is God who allows you to obtain wealth for the purpose of establishing His covenant (Deuteronomy 8:17-18). Your more comes through your dependence upon God. Your honor of Him, in the sufficiency of what you have now, is to establish His will, not yours.

Examine the following story from 1 Kings Chapter 17. God sends Elijah, the prophet, to Zarephath. There, a widow woman was commanded, by the Lord, to sustain him. During the time the prophet was sent to her, there was a great famine in the land. Interestingly, Elijah was sent to a woman who was without a husband and was poor. Despite her status, she was humble, hospitable, and obedient. The prophet asked her for a drink of water and for a morsel of bread. The woman informed him that she had just enough for herself and her son. They would eat, and then die. Clearly, she did not see the abundance in what she had.

God had already commanded there to be enough, and the abundance would come out of what was sufficient for her. Even when you do not have enough, abundance comes out of what is sufficient when you have a desire to share. In obedience to the instructions of the prophet, the widow woman demonstrated trust and dependency in God. She shared from her lack, and it became more than enough. That was evidence that God wanted more for her than what He wanted from her. Because of her sacrifice, she, her son, and the prophet ate and were satisfied many days, as the meal and oil did not run out.

This principle is not just in relation to food, money, or natural things. This also refers to how you see yourself. Understand that Sovereign God will initially place you in a lowly position first to maximize (make the best use of) you. Many want fame and prestige first, even if falsely given. "Humble yourselves in the sight of the Lord, and He shall lift you up" (James 4:10). God will cause others to honor and respect you (genuinely). The issue is, we often want more than what we have the character to sustain. As well, the heart and will, is not postured to honor God.

Many fail to see that the appointed position, whatever it maybe, is a blessing within itself. Many want the prestige and promotion of the position but lack understanding of the assignment. Understand that Jesus' position, while on earth, was as that of a lowly servant. A status the world deems as low, but God esteems high. The world wants to be served. Jesus stated and demonstrated that He did not come to be served but to serve. The world's mindset is to always want more; therefore, daily sufficiency is never enough. This mindset prevents you from seeing the blessings of sufficiency, because the outlook is limited to what self wants today.

The way of the world is to live large and acquire more than what is needed. To simply meet the need is often viewed as not having enough. That perspective may indicate a lack of contentment for what is already acquired or accomplished. Instead of honoring God for what He has already done and given, we often see behaviors or hear words that dishonor God. As a result, what should be a blessing to you and others, may cause a curse instead.

Sufficiency is always more than enough when you honor God with what you have. In that, there is no need to worry about tomorrow. We are to maximize that which is sufficient for the day. In doing so, you demonstrate trust in God, and you extract the abundance out of what is sufficient. Remember, the abundance is in your sufficiency, when it is shared. The boy shared his two fish and five loaves, the widow woman shared her meal and oil, and more importantly, God shared His Son, Jesus!

Sharing is the way to abundance. It is the heart that reveals if you have the capacity and willingness to share. Shift your thinking from viewing sufficiency as being all about you. Know that it includes having the inward desire to share. In that, the abundance is revealed. We see evidence of this in the following verses of scripture in Acts (4:32-35).

Note in verse 32, no one had the mindset that their possessions were for them alone. Their belief led to unity, which led to sharing. As a result, no one lacked anything. Please grasp, God never gives you anything that is all about you. This includes your relationship with Him, your gifts, and all you accomplish in life. Luke, 11:3 states: "Give us (not me) day by day our daily bread." Let us briefly examine the "bread," as it is important that you understand the core meaning of the bread.

ARTOS AS DIVINE PROVISION

The Greek word for bread is *artos*. *Artos* is a round cake that is approximately the size of a platter, and it is about as thick as your thumb. The Greek origin of *artos* is the word airo meaning to elevate, lift up, take upon one's self, or to carry what has been raised up. What is important about *artos* is that it was broken for the purpose of sharing. Traditionally, the Jewish people did not cut the *artos,* because to cut it symbolized separation. *Artos* is viewed as divine provision. It is the fullness of the sustenance that God gives to believers, who submit to Him, for the purpose of living to fulfill His will.

Note Jesus' conversation in St. John, 6:48-51 with the Jews concerning the bread that their fathers ate in the wilderness. In this gospel, Jesus clearly identifies Himself as the Bread of Life. Jesus makes it clear that He is representative of the bread that Israel once ate after their exodus from Egypt (see Exodus 16:1-36). In St. John 6:49, it states the fathers of Israel ate of that bread and did die.

However, in verse 50, it is noted that if anyone ate of the bread that came down from heaven, they would not die. Jesus is the true Bread of Life that came down from heaven. The bread provided in the wilderness was only a symbol of that which was to come. That bread was representative of the flesh of Jesus given for all of humanity.

Another instance in which we see the breaking and sharing of bread is in 1 Corinthians 11:23-24. The bread symbolizes the broken (shared) body of Christ given to bring us into fellowship with God. He was wounded because of our sins, crushed for our iniquities, and gave His life, so that we could live. Hence, like the *artos,* Jesus is to be shared, because He is the Bread of Life for all. Unlike the manna that provided sufficiency only for the day, Jesus is the eternal bread that gives eternal life. He is to be received, then shared.

Unfortunately, the nature of the flesh is to think only about itself. Consequently, sufficiency is not obtained. Often, the mindset is to receive provisions for the purpose of self-consumption. Remember, the scripture says, "…our daily bread." The bread is not for your sole use. It is not for you to say I got mine, now you get yours.

You are to honor God with whatever He gives you. Jesus demonstrated this when He lifted the two fish and the five loaves to heaven. He took them, blessed them, and then broke them for sharing. Give or share, and it will come back to you more abundantly.

Knowing that God gives seed to the sower and bread to the eater, understand what the seed represents. Seed is provision not yet manifested. Every seed has the potential to become provision or bread for you and others in need. For example, farmers never farm for themselves alone. Their harvest produces what they need, and the abundance is given or sold to others who have need. We find this biblical principle in Leviticus (23:22) (NIV).

When you glean (extract or collect) from the fields, leave some for the poor. Why? It is better to give, than to receive. The giver is always providing and sharing. To have a clear understanding of sufficiency, you must grasp the principle of giving and sharing. Remember St. John 3:16? God loved the world, meaning all nations, nationalities, races, and genders, so He gave the life of His Son.

God consistently gives to you, but it is never just for you, or all about you. Your life, your gifts, your experiences, and your treasures are to be shared. The more you share (give), the more you receive. Proof of this is found in Luke 6:38. When this scripture is read in the Message translation, the last portion noted is "generosity begets generosity."

Please understand, we do not give to get! We give because it is the plan and will of God. He gives to us individually. We take a portion of it to share with someone else. In sharing, you honor the Father. When you understand God and His character, you know God is what He gives, for He shares what He is!

The wealth of the life that is in you is revealed through the heart of generosity. Your life is to be shared. God's intent for your life is to produce more life. We should always want to give life, in some capacity. That is the beauty of giving. That is what *artos* is all about. Jesus gave Himself as provision for all. See yourself as provision for others.

Seeing yourself as provision for others starts within the heart. "For as he/she thinks in his heart, so is he (in behavior)" (Prov. 23:7, AMP). When you are provision, what is in you should flow out to others. You are provision or seed in the earth. Your possessions, skills, and talents are to be used for someone else, and God gets the glory. You are a gift to mankind! Life produces life when it is continually shared.

Jesus taught the disciples to pray, "...give us day by day our daily bread." At first glance, the depth and power of that request is easily missed. You hear it or read it and right away, you think that it means something just for you. That is only partially true. In the fullness of truth, it is also not just about natural bread; it is about spiritual bread.

It is not just about the physical you; it is also about the spiritual you. If only natural bread is given, you eat and are nourished for a day. When given spiritual bread, you are sustained for eternity. I remind you, Jesus is the Bread of Life given to mankind by God. Jesus was *artos* for us when He carried the cross to Calvary and gave His life.

Likewise, we become bread to the nations when we give of the life God gave us. If you have life, you have something to give. When you have nothing physical, you always have something spiritual. A kind word could stop a suicide or homicide. A word of comfort and hope can become food for the hopeless. When you genuinely give, you give life!

GIVING PRODUCES ABUNDANCE

You are not rich by what you possess. You are rich by what has been invested in you spiritually. Remember, living waters (life) should flow freely from you. You will always have more when your heart is to give. Your sufficiency is in giving and that produces your abundance.

The conclusion of this matter is this: In daily sufficiency, you must trust God to supply all that is necessary to sustain your life. Then share the life God gives you. When you are faithful (a good steward) with the little, He will manifest the more (abundance). I give you proof through my story.

As a former athlete, I was used to injuries having played basketball for many years. Typically, I would recover with no residual issues, but not this time. I developed this uncomfortable feeling in my lower right foot. I just thought I sprained it or overstretched it. I continued to play ball and continued to drive for the Chicago Transit Authority. Over time, it worsened! My foot and ankle became painful, numb, and began to turn black.

I eventually went to the doctor. After his examination, he wrote something on a piece of paper, put it in an envelope, and sealed it. With no explanation to me, he immediately sent me to a specialist. The specialist read what was written, then began his examination by putting his hand behind my right knee. He then had me put my hand behind my right knee. I could feel a pulsating sensation in my leg.

The specialist then explained that the main artery in my right leg had collapsed. This caused pain, numbness, and the black discoloration to my right ankle and foot. He stated that my lower extremity was dying due to a lack of blood flow. He then said what no one wants to hear. He said I would need surgery immediately! He also said, it was a possibility that I could lose my leg.

I left his office in disbelief! As I was driving home to tell my wife, I began to pray. Fighting tears, I remember saying, "Lord, you cannot take my leg. I have not played ball with my son. I need my leg to drive so I can provide for my family." I felt the weight of depression trying to overtake me. Suddenly, the Holy Spirit said to me, "You know the Lord!"

Immediately, my prayer shifted! Instead of pleading with the Lord to save my leg, I began declaring the word of the Lord! I remember praying healing is the children's bread just as I had prayed over my daughter. I declared, "You are the God who heals. Heal me, and I shall be healed." I went from an overwhelming depression into a radical praise!

The night before the surgery, while lying in bed, I was awakened by the Holy Spirit. He had me to turn on the television. While flipping through the channels, I came across a surgical station. I watched the story of a gentleman who had been in a motorcycle accident. It showed how they had restructured his bones, and placed pins in his legs enabling him to walk again.

The Holy Spirit assured me that the physicians had the knowledge to perform my type of surgery. He encouraged me and said that all would be well. As they had to bypass nerves and tendons to get to the artery, it was a long and tedious surgery (9-10 hours). To God be all the glory! I came through the surgery with no pain and was up walking within 24 hours. Wait, there is more!

I was off work for months, but my wife and young children were still relying on me to provide. During that time, my mortgage significantly increased! All the bills were behind! I recall my wife saying, they were depending on me to get the family back on track. I sat on my bed feeling overwhelmed, so I did what I knew to do. I took it to the Lord in prayer.

I remember praying Malachi 3:10: "Bring ye all the tithes into the storehouse, that there may be meat in mine house, and prove me now herewith, saith the Lord of hosts, if I will not open you the windows of heaven, and pour you out a blessing, that there shall not be room enough to receive it." Then I said, "Lord, I have done what you asked. I have room to receive."

The Holy Spirit then instructed me to go to my job and request a pay advance. Reluctantly, I obeyed. When I told the administrator why I was there, and what I wanted, she laughed at me. Looking as if she had seen a ghost, she came out of the office with a piece of paper in her hand. Without explanation of what was on the paper, she gave it to me, and instructed me to take it to the cashier.

I received my pay advance! An advance that to this day (many years later), I have not been asked to pay back. Then, I received a call from my father, who stated he wanted to bless me financially. Later that evening, I received a check in the mail from the mortgage company for overpayment. Shortly thereafter, my co-workers called, and stated they wanted to pay my bills for the next 3 months.

Checks continued to just show up in the mail! People would just come and bless me financially. All the while, I continued to sow! I continued to serve! I shared my life, and my testimony, every chance I was given. The abundance of the sufficiency was so much that my co-workers did not have to pay any of my bills. I even went back to work in a new car! I trusted El Roi, the God who sees, and Jehovah Jireh, the Lord who provides. He saw, met all my needs, and did exceeding, abundantly above what I asked or even thought!

It is the Father's good pleasure to give you the kingdom (Luke 12:32). The kingdom is righteousness, peace, and joy in the Holy Spirit. He takes pleasure in the prosperity of His people. He continuously gives to you, so you can share with others.

Let this principle become a part of your daily prayer and meditation. The Sovereign King knows the content and desires of your heart. He indeed can meet all your needs according to His glorious riches in Christ!

PRAYER

Abba, you are my Father, protector, keeper, and provider. Your word declares your love and care for my daily needs. Therefore, I shall not want. O true and living God, teach me how to plant seeds of life and to share the provision that it produces, so that greed does not fill my heart. I trust in your faithful guidance leading me to follow, to believe the impossible, and be in expectation of the heavenly outpour of the miraculous, in Jesus name, amen!

— Lawrence Deon Hill

CALL TO ACTION…consider the prayer guide you just read. Meditate on the example prayer then write your own personal prayer.

STRUCTURAL GUIDE #4

DEBT CANCELLATION:
THE HEART OF FORGIVENESS

Luke 11:4: And forgive us our sins; for we also forgive everyone that is indebted to us...

CHAPTER FOUR

DEBT CANCELLATION: THE HEART OF FORGIVENESS

For many, the phrase debt cancellation brings about emotional excitement. The first thought is often related to the cancellation of monetary debt. Imagine receiving a call or a letter in the mail stating your monetary obligations are completely wiped out! Or imagine checking the balance on your high-interest credit cards and your balance is zero. The level of rejoicing that would follow news like that would no doubt be difficult to describe.

Debt cancellation includes the elimination of financial responsibility. However, the core meaning of debt cancellation is far greater. Debt cancellation means to stop or put an end to the duty or obligation to pay, deliver goods, or render service. Sadly, the full depth of this principle is misunderstood, or all too often misapplied. The initial reason for which the principle of debt cancellation was instituted was not about money. It was, and still is about life!

Prior to discussing the relationship between debt cancellation and life; first, understand that the opposite of life is death. Let us also examine how we came to exist in that state. Simply put, death is the termination or cessation of life or productivity. In Romans

6:23, we are informed that "the wages or penalty of sin (anything in opposition of God's law) is death."

How then was this penalty imputed to all? Romans 5:12 notes that "...by one man sin entered into the world and death by sin; and so, death passed upon all men, for that all have sinned." We were deceitfully sold into sin and enslaved to satan thru a willful act of disobedience. Adam's transgression against God's command brought sin, and the sentence of death upon all. That one act put all in a position of owing a debt. An obligation that no human individual could ever pay.

How then is the stain of sin and the sting of death removed? There is only one way and by one person. Christ died so that all could live. By Him, our sin debt was canceled. Our balance was brought to zero. 1 Corinthians 15:22 notes it this way: "In Adam, all die, even so in Christ shall all be made alive."

In Christ we live, and it all starts with repentance and forgiveness. Therefore, it is important to have a fundamental understanding of repentance and forgiveness. Both are core messages throughout the bible. Both are essential in getting you to the place where your debts are canceled. Both are necessary to consistently cancel the debts of others. Christ's death fully paid the price for the debt we rightfully owed through sin. It was the cancellation of our debt that restored life!

To live a restored life, and experience quality of life, we must consistently choose to repent and forgive. Repentance starts with a confession of sin. It also includes a plea to God for mercy and forgiveness. It does not end there. There should be an absolute and unconditional surrender unto the Sovereign God. There must also be a complete turning away from evil or from anything contrary to the will of God. More importantly, you must turn to God!

Too often, people turn to sources other than God. It is not long before they find themselves back in the same situation or something worse. In true repentance, there is a conscious turning away from evil thoughts and practices. It includes having a changed mind, changed heart, and a sense of sincere regret and godly sorrow. There must be a genuine desire to change. There should also be commitment to the desired change.

Just being sorry may not be enough to bring about change. An apology without change, is like faith without works. In both instances, action is required. Be fully persuaded about the change that is needed. Without it, it is more probable that there will be a return to the unrighteous practices. A heart and mindset of repentance is vital to the principle of debt cancellation.

The principle of repentance is evident throughout the bible. There is not one story in the bible that you can read in which repentance is not expressed or implied. From the prophets in the Old Testament to Jesus Christ in the New Testament, we see this principle. The prophet Ezekiel called for repentance on numerous occasions (Ezekiel 14:6, 18:30, 33:11). Additionally, so did the prophets Isaiah (30:15, 44:22, 55:7) and Hosea (14:1).

The outcry of John the Baptist in the wilderness was a message of repentance. Even the public ministry of Jesus included the admonishment to "repent for the kingdom of heaven is at hand"

(Matthew 3:2, 4:17 & Mark 1:15). Having a heart of repentance is essential, as it is the way that leads to forgiveness.

FORGIVE TO LIVE

What then is forgiveness? Simply stated, to forgive means to pardon, excuse, exonerate, or release from an obligation or debt. Forgiveness was necessary, as sin was imputed to all through Adam. Romans 3:23 affirms that everyone has sinned and fallen short of God's glory. Without the forgiveness of sin, there would be no opportunity for restoration. Without restoration, there would be no life!

Imagine living forever separated from the Source and Creator of life? What quality of life would that be? The principle of forgiveness is a vital element of life, as it impacts life spiritually, physically, and psychologically. Research has shown multiple benefits for the act or actions of forgiveness. They include such things as decreasing the risks for heart attacks, lowering blood pressure, and reducing symptoms of depression and anxiety. Without forgiveness, we could not experience the rewards of debt cancellation.

Like repentance, the principle of debt cancellation, through forgiveness, is evident throughout the bible. In the Old Testament, we read about repeated cycles of sin, enslavement, repentance, forgiveness, and restoration. In the New Testament, we read about the ultimate application of debt cancellation found only through Jesus. In Christ, is the full revelation and reward of debt cancellation.

Noted in St. John 3:16, God, through the giving of His only Son, demonstrated the principle of debt cancellation. Jesus paid the price to remove the debt of our sins. He who knew no sin became sin for all (2 Cor. 5:21). How did Jesus pay our sin debt? It was done through the shedding of His blood, and the laying down of His life. By this, full payment for the penalty of the sins of mankind (past, present, and future) was made once and for all.

Through one man sin entered the world and death through sin was passed on to everyone (Rom. 5:12). In the same manner, forgiveness through Jesus came and was passed on to everyone. Now, all can receive life because of the forgiveness of the Father, through Jesus, the Son. That is debt cancellation! In that is life! Many miss that aspect of this important principle.

There is a plethora of issues that may hinder the full revelation of this principle. There are also many reasons that impede the consistent application of this principle. For this writing, I submit the following principle, which is often not discussed or taught. However, it is at the core of the issue. It is the principle of sacrifice. To forgive, thereby canceling the debt of others, involves sacrifice. Remember, the payment of sin was death. Jesus sacrificed His life so that we could live.

For us to operate in like manner, we do not shed our blood or lay down our lives literally. Our choice to forgive symbolizes our sacrifice for others as Christ sacrificed for us. What an awesome revelation to live by! We give life to ourselves and others when we choose to forgive! Because of the sacrificial aspect of forgiveness, many have difficulty with this principle. To actively take part in the redemptive work of Jesus, you must be willing to make great sacrifices!

The sacrifice of forgiveness involves discomfort. It is not done just when it is convenient or when you feel like it. Forgiveness is applied even if the offender does not ask. It is applied regardless of the response or the outcome. Think about the great pain and sufferings Christ endured for you.

He did not wait until you asked to be forgiven for your offenses. He did not wait for the opportune time. Nor did He wait until He was in the mood. No! Jesus forgave and became the sacrificial lamb before the creation of the worlds. He did it because it was necessary. He understood that if He did not, bondage and death would continue for all.

Another issue that causes many to struggle with this principle is that it involves choice. It is not about what you think. It is not predicated upon how you feel. In fact, it is the fickleness of feelings that often obstruct or prevent the application of forgiveness. You must choose to forgive those who use you, talk about you, and seek your demise. You must choose to forgive those who see you as less than a person or refuse to treat you as an equal.

You must choose to forgive those who betray your trust or mistake your kindness for weakness. To forgive, you must choose to do so! How many times must you forgive the brother who sins against you? Are you limited to the seventy times seven as mentioned in St. Matthew 18:22? Indeed not! You are to forgive every one of your brother's trespasses (St. Matthew 18:35).

You forgive as many times as necessary because you want God to forgive you for every one of your trespasses. Christ chose to forgive you, and He chose to die for you. In like manner, you must choose to do so for others. You must look for opportunities to forgive. What a blessing to know that when you forgive, you release your brother or sister from the bondage of their offenses toward you. Additionally, you break the power of satan being worked through them.

Understand that the external offense toward you is the result of something broken or missing within the offender. Your conscientious choice must be to forgive. Do this even if it is not deserved. Doing so can bring repair and restoration to what is broken or missing within them. That is why debt cancellation through forgiveness is important. God is always looking to restore what was lost or broken.

What then does forgiveness have to do with prayer? Forgiveness and prayer are intricately connected. We find evidence of this in St. Matthew 6:12 and Luke 11:4. In fact, for prayer to be effective and productive, forgiveness must be present. For prayer to ascend and be set before the heavenly Father as incense (a sweet fragrance), it must be accompanied by forgiveness.

Here is proof. St. Mark 11:25-26 notes it like this: "And when ye stand praying, forgive, if ye have ought (unsettled concerns or problems) against any: that your Father also which is in heaven may forgive you your trespasses. But if you do not forgive, neither will your Father which is in heaven forgive your trespasses." To be pardoned for your offenses, you must be willing to pardon those who offend you. For your sins to be forgiven and remembered no more, you must be willing to forgive others of their sins. For your sins to be cast into the depths of the sea and be removed as far as the east is from the west, you must do so for others.

If you choose not to forgive, neither will you be forgiven. It is plainly written in the scriptures. When you willfully choose to hold offense in your heart toward others, then Christ's sacrifice for you cannot be applied. Failure to cancel the debt of others means your debt also remains. When this principle of debt cancellation, through forgiveness, is fully understood, extending forgiveness happens more readily.

MAKE DEBT CANCELLATION A PRIORITY

Debt cancellation, through forgiveness, is high on God's list of priorities. It must also be so for those who love Him, believe Him, and choose to live according to His will. Evidence of this importance is seen in Jesus. He chose to pray, asking the Father, in Heaven, to forgive those who wrongly accused Him then crucified Him. Even after being severely scourged, and forced to carry a large wooden cross, upon which He was later nailed, Jesus sought forgiveness for the offenders. In doing so, He canceled their debt.

I am stressing this point because it is so important to comprehend. satan is your adversary and God's enemy. He does not want you to understand this. When you remain in a state where you choose not to forgive, you essentially place yourself in a state of bondage, dying, and death. However, when you choose to live in a state of forgiveness, the cancellation of debt gives you access to many God-given blessings. These include salvation, liberation, and the restoration of your royal dominion! With personal emphasis, I note again, debt cancellation is not solely about money! It is about life!

Let us briefly look at the parable of the prodigal son found in St. Luke, Chapter 15, verses 11-32. Here is the story of a young man who asked his father to give him his portion of his inheritance. It was rightfully his, but he requested it before the appointed time. After receiving his portion, he left home taking what should have been sufficient for him, and he wasted it in extravagant living. All this being contrary to the will of his father. Initially, he lived the good life, but soon the money was gone. A famine hit the land. In need but having nothing, he was forced to put himself in bondage and work feeding swine.

As no one gave food to him, he found himself at the point of needing to eat with the swine or perish with hunger. After coming to his senses (having a change of heart and mind), he thought to return home to his father. He decided to repent for his actions and ask to be taken back as a servant instead of a son. As he journeyed home, the father saw him afar off. Love and mercy caused the father to run to his son, embrace and kiss him. The father heard the humble, apologetic words of his son, and through forgiveness, canceled the debt of his son.

Forgiveness allowed reconciliation and restoration to immediately take place. The father gave his son the best robe, put a ring on his finger, shoes on his feet, and called for a great feast. The main point of this parable is found in verse 32. The son, who was once dead, is alive again. He who was once lost is found! Reconciliation between the father and son took place, and the son was restored to his rightful place in the family. That is the purpose of debt cancellation; to bring back the lost and to restore life!

Forgiveness makes all things new! It provides opportunities for new beginnings! The beauty of forgiveness is that there is no end to the fruit of forgiveness. When forgiveness is present, mercy and grace are present. Mercy opens the way for leniency and holds back the judgement that you rightfully deserve. Grace extends kindness and gives you blessings that you have not rightfully earned.

Forgiveness is perpetual! It keeps giving and keeps going from generation to generation! What God did for you, through the forgiveness of your faults and failures, you must also do for others. Without the forgiveness of sin, there would be no life! Application of this principle is not merely a recommendation or suggestion. It is a command! To forgive is to live! I repeat, to forgive is to live!

At one of the lowest points of my life, I had to remind myself of this and live it! The murder of my only son caused a hurt so deep within my soul that no words, and no one specific sound, could fully express how I felt then and at times now. Loss of a loved one, through a senseless act of violence, causes an indescribable amount of pain. It opens the door to emotions that are difficult to overcome. Especially, when you try to manage them with your own finite strength.

However, I found and continue to find healing and peace through forgiveness. This may be difficult to comprehend naturally and intellectually. I want this to be understood spiritually. I can write this with clarity and certainty of its truth because I lived it.

It was a warm summerlike evening. My wife and I had retired for the night when we received the phone call, from a relative, informing us that our son had been shot. Although I did not want it to be so, I felt in my spirit that he was gone. I drove to the hospital in silence. My wife prayed in silence, but I could still hear her. As we arrived, we were met by detectives who confirmed that he had been shot.

The family was already gathered outside. I could hear the screams of pain and disbelief. The sound of those crying, and the hysteria, was unnerving. The physician came in, and we were given the report that he had been shot in the back and was, in fact, deceased. After receiving the report, I requested to see him. As they had not yet cleaned the body, they told me it was not a good idea, but I insisted.

The walk down the hallway to that room seemed like it took forever. As I entered the room, I saw where blood had come out of various facial orifices. I saw where there was grass, dirt, and footprints on his body where people had literally trampled upon him trying to escape the gunfire. As I stood there looking down on him, I began to feel numb. I do not remember breathing. I do not even recall how I was able to remain standing. I remember how I looked into his opened eyes, while I ran my fingers through his hair.

In that moment, I saw him playing when he was a child. I saw myself holding and rocking him when he was sick. I saw how I would pray with him. This was an experience no one should have to endure. Yet... here we were. The lives of my entire family changed forever!

It took quite some time before the image of his lifeless body would stop invading my thoughts. There were even times when that scene would get stuck in my mind. It was like a broken record. There was nothing of my own doing that could pull me out of the dark hole of my emotions. It took the power and grace of God. Bearing the pain of losing him, as well as the pressure of knowing my wife held me partially responsible, caused me to feel like I was being crushed on every side.

Over the years, and for more reasons than space would allow me to note, the relationship between my son and I had deteriorated. I eventually had to ask him to leave our home. Because of his choices, there were times when our lives were in jeopardy. I had to make a difficult but very necessary decision at that time. That decision caused a significant strain on my marriage. It eventually led to a full disconnect between my wife and me. One that had not been fully resolved, even at the time when our son was murdered.

Initially, my wife found it difficult to forgive me. Thinking it would relieve my grief, I held myself responsible. It did not! Instead, it all became fuel for my anger. I found myself filled with rage. I seriously considered becoming a vigilante to take the lives of others. You know, life for life. One was taken from me, so I felt justified in thinking about taking the life of another.

I began to feel like a caged animal with no way out! Every day I had to face his death, my strained marriage, my tormented mind, and my wounded spirit. Daily I felt heart break, mines, my wife's, and my family. I thought death to those young men would be just compensation! I wanted them caught! I wanted something to happen to them while in jail! I wanted God to repay them for what they did to me, to all of us! Knowing that they would eventually suffer psychologically, physically, and ultimately die prematurely and violently, would satisfy my pain and the storm of my anger; but would it?

I found myself asking if their deaths or my taking the life of another would fix everything. I wondered if their deaths could remove what I was feeling in my heart. I was being consumed by thoughts of what if! Those constant thoughts led me to know what I needed to do. I took all my pain, and all my cares, to the Lord in prayer.

I had to go to God for divine intervention to help my wife to forgive me for our son's death. Even though it was not by my hands, or the direct result of my decision in asking him to leave our home; I needed help! I had to go to God, so I could forgive myself. I had to go to God to deal with my own torments of thinking that I was not a good father. I was tormented by thoughts that I did not try hard enough with him.

God had to remind me of how I tried to help him and steer him in the right direction. I even came to understand that a portion of my own anger was the result of the anger my wife held toward me. I knew it was not my fault. But as a man, husband, and father, I believed that the well-being of the family was my responsibility. They depended on me. I was heavily burdened. I had to release myself from the thoughts of failure, shame, and guilt that was trying to consume me.

FORGIVE TO BE FORGIVEN

And this is where it got real: I had to forgive the individuals who murdered my son. I am a man of faith. I believe whole heartedly in the word and power of God. But this was indeed a challenge for me. Justifiably so, I had serious issues against those individuals. However, to be forgiven, I had to forgive them.

Through consistent prayer and meditation, as well as the ministry work of the Holy Spirit, all that was tormenting me was annihilated! The fight was not with my wife, my son, me, or the individuals that took the life of my son. Ephesians 6:12 tells us specifically who or what we fight against. "We wrestle not against flesh and blood, but against principalities, against powers, against the rulers of the darkness of this world, and against spiritual wickedness in high places."

It was the enemy who did not want me to forgive. Why? Because he did not want me to operate in my royal dominion! He wanted to keep me bound because that would have kept all connected to me bound. He wanted me in a place where the work of Jesus could not be applied to my life. When you choose not to forgive, you cannot and will not walk in the fullness of the liberating power of Jesus Christ.

It was by divine revelation that I came to know and eradicate the demons that sought to hold me in captivity. I had to forgive and not hold anything against my wife, my son, myself, or the ones who were responsible for his death. Understand that although I forgave, it did not change the circumstances. Neither did it remove the memories or pain of the experience. I am grateful that it did remove the torment in my mind, and the burden in my spirit.

That is the debt cancellation of Jesus! That is what He wants all men to experience. Debt cancellation gives us the ability to overcome the greatest challenges that we experience on this side of heaven. I implore you, never pass up the opportunity to forgive another of their offense. No matter how tragic, or how badly you were betrayed or hurt. Always choose to forgive!

One act of forgiveness has the potential to change not only the life of the forgiver and the offender, but it can change generations. Just as generations can be negatively affected by an offense, when generations are changed through forgiveness, history is changed also. When history is changed, the world is changed. That is exactly what happened for us when Jesus hung on the cross as a mediator between God and man. He pardoned our sins, canceled our debts, and changed the history of humanity forever!

I earnestly ask you to cancel the debts of those who have wronged you. Release them from the penalty of their transgressions. Then allow God to remove all the hurt and pain of the experience. Choose to forgive in your heart and demonstrate love through your actions. Remember, at the heart of debt cancellation is the willingness and the ability to forgive. The perfect plan of God for all of humanity includes forgiveness. Living life with a heart always ready to forgive, enables you to experience the fullness of your liberty in Christ.

Pause here and write down the names of all who may have hurt or offended you. Then as a part of your daily communication with the Heavenly Father, release a prayer of forgiveness like the one noted here as an example.

PRAYER

Father, God, strengthen me in my pursuit to forgive. I cannot accomplish this task alone. But with your Spirit helping me, I can and shall succeed. I acknowledge that at times I struggle with forgiving those who hurt me. I desire to experience the liberating power of Jesus Christ. Teach me, O God, how to let go of my past hurts and embrace my glorious future. I now prophesy over my own life, that through Jesus, I am empowered to forgive, in Jesus name, amen!

– Lawrence Deon Hill

CALL TO ACTION...consider the prayer guide you just read. Meditate on the example prayer, then write your own personal prayer.

STRUCTURAL GUIDE #5

SPIRITUAL NAVIGATION:

GUIDED FROM WITHIN

Luke 11:4...And lead us not into temptation; but deliver us from evil.

CHAPTER FIVE

SPIRITUAL NAVIGATION: GUIDED FROM WITHIN

In preparation for writing this section about spiritual navigation, I sifted through my many self-reflections and God-given revelations regarding this principle. As I did, I had this thought: There is nothing worse than being lost! With that recurring thought, a flood of emotions rushed in as my mind replayed a childhood experience. One that I vividly recall to this day.

I was about 8 years old at the time, and it was a beautiful day outside. The weather was perfect, not too hot, and not too cold. Although I had been to the zoo before, I remember being excited about my class taking a field trip to the zoo! This was back during the time when we did not have all the creative tools like child leashes or safety harnesses to keep your child connected to you so they could not get lost. At that time, all we had were the stern instructions of our parents before we left home. In addition, we had the instructions of the teacher, who strongly admonished us to stay close and not wander off.

On that day, there were so many people out, but all I thought about was the things I wanted to see! All I thought about was what

I hoped to experience! All I thought about was me, myself, and I. Although it was not my intent to become separated from my class, my innate curiosity caused me to move when I should have remained in place with my class. I was given specific instructions, but I chose to do something different. My own personal interests caused me to leave my designated place of safety and protection.

That one choice, made in that one moment of time, caused me to wander off and become separated from my class. I recall the intense, overwhelming emotions that came over me once I realized I was no longer with my assigned group. I felt afraid and helpless! My chest was heavy! I felt like I could not breathe! Panic set in! I quickly turned in circles looking in every direction trying to find my teacher and my classmates. I wanted to get back to the place I was supposed to be!

I was filled with fear and could not speak! Tears flowed from my eyes as I walked as fast as my 8-year-old legs could carry me. Frantically looking around, I remember thinking; I am lost! I will never find them, and they will never find me! I will never get home! It appeared to be hundreds, if not thousands of people all around me. Yet, I felt like I was all alone, and there was no one to help me. Then I heard this sweet, soft, calming voice say, "Are you lost?" All I could do was shake my head up and down to indicate that I was lost.

The stranger took my small hand and placed it in hers. She softly said to me, "I will help you." I was terrified! I was lost, and my only source of help was someone I did not know. I felt ashamed for what I had done. But in that moment, the kind act of a total stranger wrapping her hand around mine caused me to feel safe. I felt a sense of peace because there was someone to comfort, help, and guide me.

As we began to walk together, she was leading, and I followed. It was not long before the path we were walking led us to my teacher. My teacher was looking for me, just as we were looking for her. Once I clearly saw her, I ran to her, wrapped my arms around her, and held on tight! I cried, not because I was lost; I cried because I was found! I cried because I was restored to my rightful place! I cried because I was now back in my appointed position!

Although I was the one who disobeyed clear instructions, my teacher recognized the innocence of my act. She saw my expressed appreciation of being reconciled with my class. It was evident that I had learned a great lesson. So instead of discipline, she showed mercy and embraced me back. The return embrace assured me that I was indeed safe. For the remainder of that trip, I stayed close. I did not become separated from my class or move from my assigned position again.

The lesson of that experience revealed that when you are led solely by the emotions of what you desire or think you want or need; it is easy to go off course. It is easy to become lost. Particularly, if you are in a large crowd. Often, no one notices initially because everyone is focused on themselves. They are focused on the outcomes of what they want.

When you find yourself off-track and wandering, whether it is innocently unintentional, or it is done in selfish and intentional disregard, the Holy Spirit is a present help. He is there to usher you back to your rightful place. The place of unbroken fellowship with the Father. My childhood experience reminded me of that.

It also brought to life the parable of the lost sheep. That story is found in St. Luke, Chapter 15. Jesus tells a parable about a man who had 100 sheep but loses one. He left the 99 to search for the one until he found it. After finding the one lost sheep, the man joyfully returns home and calls for a celebration. Likewise, Jesus goes on to say there will be more joy in heaven over one who repents (who turns and comes back or is led back) than over the 99 that does not need to repent. In other words, when what was missing is recovered or brought back, there is great joy!

I shared all that to lay a foundation for the discussion regarding spiritual navigation. Today, many are lost and do not know it or understand why. Often, they are not even aware that they have gone astray. Like I was as a child, many are unaware that they have been led astray by external influences, or by their own inner desires. Or like when Adam's desires and decisions caused him to become separated from the Heavenly Father.

Once the distraction leads you off course, it is easy to then lose focus. You lose sight of the original goal or purpose. There is a loss of direction, and you may end up going in circles. Although this principle is mentioned last, it is of critical importance. In fact, this principle must be used to undergird all the others. It provides the necessary foundation and support to advance through the various realms and dimensions of prayer.

As we continue the discussion of spiritual navigation, keep in mind that whatever or whoever influences you will ultimately lead you. Whether it is the latest trends, your friends, what others say, how you feel, what you have read, or what you have experienced. These ever-changing factors can cause you to make irreversible, irreparable, and sometimes permanent decisions for temporary circumstances.

For that reason, the surest way to stay on course is to be led by God. We are reminded that "the very steps we take come from God; otherwise, how could we know where we are going (Prov. 20:24, Message)?" As we travel the roads of life, we should have a sense of direction. There should be an intended destination. Without them, you may end up lost. You are more vulnerable when you have no one to lead, guide, and support you.

Now, pause for a moment and imagine this: you go on vacation to a foreign country or a place you have never visited before. No doubt, along with the excitement of seeing new things and gaining new experiences, there would be some anxiety or apprehension. You are cautious, because you may not know exactly who to talk to, or what you should be doing, as you are trying to figure out the best places you should go.

GUIDANCE ENSURES ARRIVAL

Also, imagine trying to get somewhere without a definitive sense of purpose or direction. That would be like going somewhere and you do not know why you are going. Or maybe you go just for the sake of going. In not knowing your way around a particular area, it is then beneficial to have someone or something to safely guide you. Proper guidance ensures that you get to your intended destination.

Otherwise, without proper guidance you would be lost; right? Who, in their sound mind, would choose to be lost and remain lost? Only the ignorant would choose that. If you are reading this book, that is not you! To sufficiently guide you, that someone or something would have to be familiar with where you are trying to go. If they are unfamiliar, it would be like the blind leading the blind. The bible clearly tells us what happens when the blind lead the blind; they both fall into the ditch (Matt. 15:14).

To avoid such a fall, you should know the location of the ditch, or at least have someone to guide you around it. Providing guidance and direction is what a tour guide would do. That is also what the global positioning system (GPS) does for those who activate it for travel purposes. Both assist you to get where you are going and navigate you in, through, and around that which is unfamiliar.

That is what spiritual navigation is about. Getting you where you are appointed to be and guiding you through what you are anointed to do. It helps you to go from faith to faith and glory to glory in the spirit. Therefore, understand this as the strategic movement of the believer. Its purpose is to help you avoid the traps and snares set by satan to delay, deny, derail, and ultimately destroy you.

It is through divine guidance that you can strategically maneuver through the various dimensions and realms of the spirit. Streetlights and signs provide guidance in terms of who should be moving, who should be stopped, or who should proceed with caution; correct? Like streetlights and signs, spiritual navigation helps you to know when to move and when to remain still. It helps to determine your current position. It helps you to plan for your next course of movement or action.

It helps you to know how far you have gone and how much farther you need to go. It provides insight about where you have been. It also confirms if you are going in the right direction. It will inform you when you are off course and need to turn around, change, or adjust your course of movement. It opens the door for enlightenment as you travel the roads of life. Above all, you are provided with the instructions and strategies that help your prayers break through demonic barriers to ultimately penetrate the heavens.

Being guided spiritually is of vital importance to the believer. Without it, you may end up in the wrong place, wasting time, or doing the wrong thing. You may miss experiencing or obtaining what has already been prepared and predestined just for you. For those reasons, the significance of this principle must not be underestimated or minimized.

Just because you confess Christ as Savior, or you possess spiritual gifts that does not mean you readily know where you are going. It does not mean you readily know what to do with the gifts you have been given. The gifts and callings of God are without repentance. They are irrevocable (Rom. 11:29). Although you have an awesome gift in your ability to make choices, God wants to lead you. As He led Adam, He wants to lead you!

Remember the first man Adam? He was initially led by God. He was given dominion over the fish of the sea, the fowl of the air, over the cattle, over all the earth, and over every creeping thing (Gen 1:26). He was then placed in the Garden of Eden to guard and keep it. Adam was also directed not to eat of the tree of the knowledge of good and evil. To do so would result in death, not physically but spiritually. The God-given authority and instructions given to Adam may be considered as the bible's first recorded example of spiritual navigation involving mankind.

As you continue to read about Adam, you discover that he did not adhere to the directives he was given. His disobedience resulted in what we refer to as the fall of man. What was so significant about the fall of man? It was then that Adam lost His spiritual connection and perception. His sin, made by his free-will choice, caused him to be out of his divinely appointed position. He lost His spiritual compass. Because of that, he tried to hide from God. Adam's choice, to be led by something other than God, negatively affected him, mankind, and all of creation.

Like Adam, there are many people who make decisions based on how they feel, what they want, or how they think. Many will trust and rely on their own intellect, personal talents, abilities, and instincts. Too often, there are those who make choices being influenced by the emotions of that one moment. Which one are you? Prayerfully none! I admonish you to be mindful and not allow yourself to be consistently identified in either of those categories.

That type of self-empowerment and self-guidance will cause you to move out of position. It causes a malfunction in your spiritual compass. It weakens your connection to the very source of life. Instead of drawing near to God, it causes you to draw back from God. Self-sufficiency and self-reliance are in direct opposition to the core meaning of spiritual navigation.

When you depend on self, you fail to do what you are admonished to do in Proverbs 3:5-6 (Message), which is to trust God from the bottom of your heart. You are not to try to figure out anything on your own. You are to listen for God's voice (His instructions) in all you do and everywhere you go. He alone is the one who will keep you on track and going in the right direction.

When you are being guided spiritually, you cannot rely on your own understanding. You must trust and have faith in God alone. In St. John, Chapter 10, we read that those who belong to God know His voice and follow Him and the voices of strangers they do not follow. Just as the GPS sends it signals to the intended mode of transportation to direct you to your intended destination; likewise, it is so in Christ. He leads and guides you by His Holy Spirit. It is up to you to follow Him.

You must accept and submit to the instructions you are given. You cannot do it your way. You must obey the Lord's commands. It is often a challenge to trust God and not depend upon self. Self can cause one to feel right and justified in their thoughts and actions. We are warned, however, about trusting the way that appears to be right and seemingly harmless, because its end is destruction or even death (Proverbs 14:12).

One of the many challenges with being divinely directed is that most people do not like being told what to do. Therefore, they do not seek counsel until they are already drowning in trouble. They often just want what they want, when and how they want it. They give no regard to the end results, or its obvious negative consequences. This type of self-serving mindset can be seen in everyday life. It was first seen in the Garden of Eden with Adam and Eve.

In Genesis, Chapter 3, the serpent poses a question to Eve that he already knew the answer to. He asked, "Has God indeed said, 'You shall not eat of every tree of the garden'?" In response, Eve clearly articulated to the serpent that she and Adam could freely eat of the trees in the garden. The only exception was for the one tree that sat in the middle of the garden. She further stated, they could not eat of it, touch it, or they would die.

Appealing to her sense of self and the desire for self-gratification, the serpent was able to deceive Eve. He told her, "You shall not surely die." Perceiving the tree to be good for food, pleasing to look at, and desirable for gaining wisdom, she did indulge. She also shared with her husband. What was the result of their self-serving decision? It was death, not physically but certainly spiritually and psychologically.

Understand that spiritual navigation is not just about telling you what to do, when to do it, or how to do it. Neither is it just about giving a bunch of rules and regulations with its resulting consequences. Its primary purpose is to assist you in the strategic access and use of all the resources of heaven. It will help you to go through the various seasons and cycles of life wisely, successfully, and victoriously.

GOD WANTS TO LEAD YOU

Without adequate guidance, it can be difficult to discern right from wrong. It is more likely you will become distracted and end up off course. It is also more likely that your prayers will be hindered. You may end up wandering in the wilderness of life.

Particularly, if you choose to live independent of your Creator. Remember, God wants to lead you!

That is the most important aspect of this principle. You are led. You are led of the Lord, by His Holy Spirit! In Psalms 32:8 (NLT), He says, "I will guide you along the best pathway for your life. I will counsel (advise) you and watch over you." We are to walk with God and allow Him to lead us. It is written for our learning that Enoch walked with God, indicating that God led him. To walk with God, you must follow the lead of God.

You cannot and should not be in front of God. Neither should you try to cleverly steer God in the direction you want. Your position must always be that of a follower. You are to be a devoted disciple. What He commands, you do. Where He leads, you go. What He says, you accept. However, be aware that as God leads you, He may shift His position.

Recall the events of the children of Israel, after they left Egypt, and they found themselves facing the Red Sea in front of them and Pharaoh's army behind them. We read that God had gone before them to guide them. When it was necessary to do so, He went behind them to protect them.

He is still able and will do the same for you today! Fully submit your ways to God. Accept and agree with His will. Then it is possible for Him to walk alongside of you, in front of you, or behind you depending on your need. Through your covenant relationship with the Father, He makes known His various positions. You can trust that He will not leave you, regardless of the state you find yourself in. Though you may not always see or feel Him, remain confident in His ability to instruct you.

Do that by relying on His unfailing promises. Reliance on God's infallible word is critical to the believer. The sons of God are led by the Spirit of God (Rom. 8:14). I know this is the opposite of the world's many changing mantras. The world says, go your own way, be your own boss, do your own thing, and have it all your own way!

I implore you to lay hold of this truth: God alone knows the plans that He has for you. His plans for you are good, not evil, and they give you a future and an expected end (Jere. 29:11). To successfully live according to His plans, you must adhere to His directives. His way must supersede your way!

Another point to note is this, spiritual navigation is a concept spiritually discerned and understood. It may not always look like the right place or the right thing in the natural. It may not always feel right. Just remember, you are led of the Lord, by His Spirit. Never be led by feelings alone. Feelings can be deceptive due to their ever-changing nature. Feelings can be influenced by what looks, sounds, or feels right, but may not be right, or be grounded in any truth.

You are a spirit being. You live in a house of flesh (the body). You must maneuver through an ever-evolving natural world. Therefore, you must be led and guided by the Lord. To see God's kingdom and consistently experience His will, you must adhere to His commands. That goes back to the principle noted in St. Luke 11:2.

It is critical that you understand that in every situation, no matter how great or small, you are to allow God to lead you! Whether it is in ministry, business, related to family, or something personal, be led by the Lord. Even in those areas where you previously made your own choices and experienced success, still allow God to guide you. Just because you did it before, and it worked, does not mean it will happen that way all the time.

That is why, as a people, we look to Him when we make decisions or come to a crossroad. If we always knew where to go and what to do, it would not have been necessary for us to be reminded to acknowledge the Lord. Understand that living your best life is not about how you feel. It is about His will for your life. The word of the Lord says this, "Cursed is the man that trusts in man (or draws strength from the flesh meaning himself) and whose heart turns from the Lord," but "Blessed is the man that trusts in the Lord and has confidence in Him" (Jere. 17: 5 & 7).

With that in mind, imagine what might have happened to Israel as they journeyed through the wilderness? Imagine them being moved by what they saw instead of remaining yielded to the pillar of cloud by day, and the pillar of fire by night. They were indeed guided by a supernatural compass with tangible manifestations.

What could have happened had they relied on their own abilities and strength? What would have been their fate had they gone their own way? What may have occurred had their trust been in man alone? Recall, Pharaoh's army was aggressively pursuing them from behind, while they faced the Red Sea in front of them. Doing it their own way would have certainly resulted in defeat, captivity, or death.

It was their trust in God and remaining under His guidance and protection that ensured their victory. Even in the presence of fear, they trusted God. That story confirms for us that we are to walk by faith and not by sight. Why? Because we are led by the Spirit of the Living God!

I am sure, by now, you know that the one who leads is the Holy Spirit. He is the third and distinct person of the Holy Trinity. He is God's active power here in the earth. He operates in our lives as life and breath. God breathed into man the breath of life. That breath is His Spirit connecting with the life within us to reconnect us to God. We were never created to be independent and live apart from our Creator. The Holy Spirit enables God to live with and in us to teach and guide us.

From Genesis to Revelation, we can read about the works of the Holy Spirit. The Holy Spirit was present and active in creation (Gen 1:1). The Holy Spirit was also vital to Christ's earthly ministry. Jesus did not fully begin His ministry works until He was endowed with the Holy Spirit. As it was for our Savior, so it is for us in every aspect of our lives. This is especially so in prayer.

To pray without the help of the Holy Spirit is like a car without gas. We can get in the car, but we will not get far, if we get anywhere at all. Prayer without the assistance of the Holy Spirit is also like a power cord unplugged from the electrical power source; it is useless. To persevere, prevail, and ascend in prayer, we need the aide of the Holy Spirit. Romans 8:26 tells us why: we do not always know what we should pray for, but the Holy Spirit intercedes for us with inarticulate sounds too deep for words.

There is much that can be said about the roles and functions of the Holy Spirit, in the lives of mankind. So much so, that it would require writing another volume of books. In short, He is comforter, helper, intercessor, and guide. He is the conduit by which the unseen becomes seen. He reveals the heart and will of God. He assists you to be able to relate to a Holy God. He equips you to fulfill the purpose for which you have been given life. He helps you to do what you cannot do on your own.

He is God's limitless power at work within, around, and through you. His work is not to make you dance, run around the building, and fall out. He is not your genie in a bottle to grant you unlimited wishes. His work is not to ensure that your unique brand of ministry is known around the world. He is not something you have to wait for or try to catch. He is a gift to be received!

Your acceptance of Him enables Him to watch over you as a shepherd takes care of sheep. He, then, will not have to drive you like a cowboy drives cattle. The Holy Spirit does not force Himself into your life as a trespasser. Nor does he break in like a thief breaking into your home. He waits for your welcome! Then He comes into your life with the primary function to guide you into all truths.

In the 16th Chapter of St. John, Jesus makes known why it is to your advantage that He went away. Had He remained, the Holy Spirit could not come to illuminate and make known the things of God. The Holy Spirit does not boast of Himself for personal fame. He glorifies Christ! He makes known all that Christ has already said and established. In knowing Christ, the Son, we know God, the Father. The Son was the visible representation of the invisible God. That is the work of the Holy Spirit: He points to Christ and Christ points to the Father.

I pause here and ask; do you believe that you have or will receive salvation? In addition, have you received the gift of the Holy Spirit since you believed? Both are equally important. Receiving the gift of salvation is the initial step. Being guided spiritually is another aspect of this ongoing relational process.

FATHERED & LED BY GOD

Those who are fathered by God are also guided by God. God does not father whom He cannot guide. If He is not consistently guiding you, He is not fathering you. I suggest to you, it is far better to be guided from above (spiritually) than to be led from below (naturally). If God is fathering you, you should have complete trust and total dependency on Him. Allow Him to guide you by the unseen, as that is what faith is. It allows you to know that you are sustained from above, because you are fathered from above.

This understanding gives access for the Holy Spirit to navigate you along your life's journeys. Submitting to the directives of God, and allowing Him to go before you, must become a consistent way of thinking and living. If you confess Christ as Lord, then no decision or movement should be made without guidance.

It is in Him we live, move, and exist or have our being (Acts 17:28). Every act and action should be in, with, and through Him. God wants to guide all aspects of your life. It is necessary to reach certain realms of glory. It ensures your journey ends back in the eternal place with God. As you go through this pilgrimage called life, being navigated spiritually is a must!

Why is it a must? In our current natural state, we must contend with the desires of the flesh (sensual desires, passions, & all types of hunger), the desires of the eyes (especially covetousness), and the pride of life (desire for power & superiority) (1 John 2:16). The appetite for physical pleasure, and the need to satisfy all its longings, is why we need the help and guidance of the Holy Spirit.

Therefore, as part of our daily bread, we pray the words noted in St. Luke 11:4: "…lead us not into temptation; but deliver us from evil," or from the evils of the evil one. This is an important supplication. satan is continuously on the prowl seeking whom he may devour or destroy completely. He uses various schemes, tactics, and ploys to tempt us. Temptation is the person or situation placed before you to get you to leave one condition or position and move into another. It is also representation of a false climate built upon prevailing public opinions and trends.

That is significant, as they often affect what you do and how you do it. Temptation can and will place you in an attitude or posture that is not agreeable with God's plans for your life. Through various types of temptations, satan attempts to get you to do something outside of what you should be doing. Especially, if that something is wrong or considered immoral.

The tempter, satan, is an opportunist, who looks for reasons and seasons to strip you of what God has appointed for you. He entices you with what only appears to be good and right. He works to get you to move out of your divine state to operate from your mortal state. The mortal state being a condition or position that is subject to death. Remember, the wages of sin is death. The end goal of temptation is to get you to sin.

The objective of sin is to get you to commit an offense against yourself, someone else, and more importantly, against God. Sin leads and drives you out of your rightful position. It can lead to separation between you and God. That supports the plan of the enemy, which is to steal, kill, and destroy. This is opposite the abundant life, which is made available only in Christ.

It is the diabolical plans of satan that makes the plea of St. Luke 11:4 important. There are some desires (true love, godly success, etc.) that are not wrong. However, when influenced by the enemy, they become subject to sin. They become an open door for evil. Evil defined as that which is sinful, morally reprehensible, or relating to bad character or conduct. Sadly, due to the heart of some, every evil may not be considered as blatantly offensive or immoral. But know this, the intent of evil is to steal life.

Evil spelled backward is live! Habitual evil practices eventually result in a loss of life. Anything that strips you of the plans, purposes, and the abundant life as intended by God, should be considered evil! Pray, then, to discern if there be any evil intent. Especially, if the intent is to steal quality of life. It is imperative to avoid becoming a victim of your own desires or the devices of the enemy. Christ's encounter with satan, in the wilderness, is a great illustration of this portion of scripture and this principle overall.

Before continuing with the discussion of Christ's wilderness encounter, I pause to note that God does not tempt anyone to sin. In fact, the tempter was identified in the previous paragraph. In James 1:13-15, we are given a clear explanation of what occurs when someone is tempted. "Let no one say when he is tempted, I am being tempted by God, for God cannot be tempted with evil, and He Himself tempts no one. But each person is tempted when he is lured and enticed by his own desire. Desire when it has conceived gives birth to sin, and sin when it is fully grown brings forth death" (ESV).

Of course, death is not always physical, and it is not always immediate. But the end of sin is certain. 1 Corinthians 10:13 provides further insight and resolution. It states: "No temptation (not one) has over-taken you except such as is common to man (others have experienced them too); but God is faithful, who will not suffer you to be tempted beyond what you are able (beyond your ability); but with the temptation will also make the way of escape that you may be able to bear (endure) it."

Your adversary will lead you into all forms of bondage (spiritually, mentally, & physically), but God always has the way out. We escape through the knowledge and application of His word and through fervent prayer. Whatever the situation that you find yourself in, God will lead you around and through it. That is spiritual navigation! The question then is not how you got there. We know choices, be it yours or someone else's, is usually the how. The greater question is how to get through and out.

While God does not lure you into sinful acts or practices, He does and will allow the trying of your faith. This is necessary. It is the trying of your faith that produces patience, promotes growth, endurance, and perseverance (James 1:3). Now, on to the narrative about Christ's wilderness encounter with satan, and how it exemplifies spiritual navigation.

The very first verse of St. Luke, Chapter 4, lets us know this meeting between Christ and satan is a clear example of spiritual navigation. It states, "Jesus, being full of the Holy Spirit returned from Jordan, and was led by the Spirit into the wilderness." Did you see it? Jesus was filled with and led by the Holy Spirit into the wilderness for the encounter with satan. He was intentionally led into a situation to be tried by the devil.

Jesus, after being baptized, heard the Father say, "This is my beloved Son in whom I am well pleased" (Matt. 3:17). The question is, why was Jesus deliberately ushered into the wilderness to be tested? Why would the Father allow His Son to be led into a hostile conflict? Why permit a confrontation with someone whose objective was to cause an abortion of purpose and forfeiture of destiny?

Why allow an experience that could bring destruction or death, not only to him but all of mankind? Hebrews 4:15 gives the answer: "For we have not a high priest which cannot be touched with the feeling of our infirmities; but was in all points tempted like as we are, yet without sin" (KJV). Jesus is quite familiar with all our infirmities. In His humanity, Jesus was aware of our human struggles. He was exposed to and experienced life challenges, just like anyone else. Yet, He was able to overcome them without committing sin.

The purpose of that encounter was to give us a clear picture of Jesus. He laid aside His divinity to become our High Priest. In doing so, He became acquainted with all the desires, temptations, and weaknesses of the flesh. He showed us how to live with and overcome them. In the wilderness account, satan attempted to lure

Jesus with the lust of the flesh, the lust of the eyes, and the pride of life (Luke 4:3-13). All of these were and still are issues common to humanity.

By His Spirit, you have the power to overcome ungodly desires and weaknesses of the flesh. Having the ability to conquer and subdue the temperaments of the flesh, through Christ, abolishes the age-old excuse, "This is just the way I am." No, it is how you choose to be. It shows that you conveniently choose to disregard the fact that Christ overcame all human faults, flaws, and frailties common to man.

In Him, you can too! If God allows the trial or leads you to it, trust that He will navigate you through it. Psalms 34:19 makes it known that the afflictions (pain and sufferings) of the righteous will be many, but He will deliver (save, rescue) you out of them all. In this natural life, you will be tried and tempted. Some will be the result of your choices. Others may be divinely orchestrated. In either case, they are not for you to fail.

Their intent is to mature you. They allow you to gain better insight of yourself. They become the opportunities for you to successfully maneuver through life. Sovereign God already knows what negative events you will have to experience. The help through them, and the solutions for them, were already provided. He already knows who and what will be a part of your life experiences. You must trust that He is a present help. He has overcome all that is in the world, and so can you, when led by His Spirit!

TRUST GOD

The wilderness account makes it clear that if God allows it, He is more than able to lead you around or through it. Christ's wilderness victory is undeniable evidence that what God did, by His Spirit, for His only Son, He will also do for those who trust and are led by Him. Will you trust God to navigate you through your wilderness journeys? Will you trust God to lead you through seasons where you feel inadequate, neglected, rejected, or abandoned? Will you permit Him to guide you through your moments of uncertainty? Will you allow Him to help you gain victory over every deceitful enticement of satan?

These are questions to consider and develop answers to. Job 5:7 tells us that "Yet man is born unto trouble" and likewise, Job 14:1 states, "Man that is born of a woman is of few days and full of trouble." Do not be alarmed! Christ overcame all that is in the world, for you!

The moment you open your eyes and get out of bed, activate your spiritual navigation system (SNS). Do not leave home, go to work, engage family, friend, or foe without invoking the assistance of your Helper. And certainly, do not attempt to make any decisions without this system being fully activated!

Just as the GPS knows the traffic patterns and tries to maneuver you around the sites of congestion, construction, and accidents, so does the Holy Spirit know what you will face every day. He seeks to lead you around it all. The evil one lies in wait with his schemes seeking whom he may distract and destroy. By the Holy Spirit, you can be routed around and through it. You can even ascend above it in prayer. Whereas the GPS may fail, as its technology is dependent upon man, the SNS (ordained of God) never fails!

I implore you to be empowered by the Holy Spirit! Learn to skillfully use the word of God. Jesus showed us how in the wilderness encounter. We pray to not be led into temptation. In the event we are, we then pray for deliverance. God's word, and the Holy Spirit, help us to avoid or overcome the destructive plans of satan.

With them, we can break through demonic interference. We can minimize the delaying tactics of the evil one. We can see beyond what is seen. We can be re-routed around satanic barriers, minimize the loss of time, or redeem time already lost. We must faithfully activate our spiritual navigation system!

This system needs no upgrade. It is user friendly and available in all languages. It will never become obsolete! It just makes sense to be led by the one who already knows your end from your right now. It really is more advantageous to trust in the one whose thoughts and ways are more superior in comparison to yours or anyone else's. Unfortunately, many fear the loss of control and therefore, resist being led. Having a clear understanding of the intent of divine guidance should remove all fear, and the sense of loss of self-control.

The purpose of being spiritually guided is not for the sole purpose of control. In fact, you always have a choice to submit and follow. Or you can rebel and endure the consequences. Recall, that the primary purpose of spiritual navigation is to assist you in the strategic access and use of all the resources of heaven. Why? So that you can then wisely, successfully, and victoriously go through the various seasons and cycles of life. It helps to build your trust in God. It matures your faith.

By faith, engage and activate your SNS. Like Christ did in the wilderness, depend on the Holy Spirit to assist you in the proficient use of the word of God. When the enemy says sick, you remind him by whose stripes you are healed (Isaiah 53:5). When he says bound, remind him that you are indeed free (John 8:36). When he says die, remind him that you will not die but live and declare the works of the Lord (Psalms 118:17). It is the word of truth that successfully activates and navigates you through the life you have been given to live.

Remember, we cannot know truth except the Spirit of Truth makes known what is true. It is God's word alone that is truth. His word does not and will not fail. In prayer, activate your SNS to reach your appointed destination at the appointed time both naturally and spiritually. It is through spiritual navigation that you will not only send up prayer, but you will ascend in prayer.

This principle must be a part of your daily communication with God. Remember, it is He who knows and has the perfect plans for your life. He knows the paths that you should take to ensure their fulfillment. Therefore, daily ask for His guidance. Always trust in His authority and ability to lead you. I charge you to activate your SNS daily!

Read the following example, then write your own prayer of guidance.

PRAYER

Eternal God, you are my heart's compass guiding me by your loving Spirit to keep me from going astray. O Father, you are omniscient, knowing the paths that I should take. So, order my steps and let your word guide my feet away from the traps that the devil has set for me. Help me, so I do not trust in my fleshly desires alone. Purify my emotions that I may be strong in the truth of your word. This day, I shall sing aloud your praise, because you delivered me from the kingdom of darkness, and you delivered me even from myself. Lord, I thank you in Jesus name, amen!

– Lawrence Deon Hill

CALL TO ACTION... consider the prayer guide you just read. Meditate on the example prayer, then write your own personal prayer.

ASCENSION:

THE FINAL DESTINATION

Revelations 8:4 And the smoke of the incense, which came with the prayers of the saints, ascended up before God out of the angel's hand.

CONCLUSION

ASCENSION: THE FINAL DESTINATION

Since God is omnipresent in that He is always everywhere, why do we need to ascend or go up to commune with Him? Could we just communicate from wherever we are? Could we just say what we wanted to say to Him regardless of what was going on around us? You could, but just as there are barriers in the natural that disrupt and interfere with clear communication, so it is in the spirit. The barriers must then be removed. Or you must find a way to navigate through, around, or over them. This is necessary so that the connection remains strong, and the intended exchange occurs without unnecessary delays.

Removing obstacles, as well as, including the instructions noted in the conclusion of chapter one, is key to ensuring ascension. Call to mind that you were admonished to give your undivided attention. You are to create an atmosphere conducive for fellowship with a Holy King. You are to always enter His presence with a heart of humility, thanksgiving, and worship.

Ascension must be a desired outcome of prayer. There are certain places in God and specific things about Him that will not be known or experienced unless we rise higher. Somethings are not revealed in the low place. That is the place where things are temporal or solely sensual, relating only to the here and now. There are things that cannot be made known to the carnal, immature, or self-centered mind. There are things that will not be made known to the one who is prideful, self-righteous, and interested only in receiving but not giving or sharing.

To share in the divine nature of Christ, you must go up! To be privy to the mysteries of heaven, you must shift from the natural to the supernatural. Of course, it is not possible for the physical body to ascend. However, through impassioned prayer, your spirit can rise to visit and dwell in the heavens. What does it mean then to ascend? Simply stated, it is the act of rising or moving in an upward fashion. It may also be viewed from the perspective of changing from one position to another. Specifically, from a lower position to a higher one.

It includes movement from the ordinary to the extra-ordinary places. It also involves movement from sickness to health and from poverty to wealth. From brokenness to wholeness, as well as, from sorrow and mourning to joy. Even more, it enables you to progress from the outer court into the most holy of holy places. You rise above negative circumstances. You rise above carnal mindsets. Most importantly, you rise to the standards of a Holy and Righteous God.

ASCEND IN PRAYER

Ultimately, the ascent in prayer brings you into God's presence and draws you close to His heart. Imagine being in the position of

John the disciple, sitting right next to Jesus and laying your head on His bosom. God desires that type of intimate fellowship with you. He longs for and asks you to come up and commune with Him. Prayer is the meeting place that grants you direct access to the very heart of God. For these reasons, the desire to go higher must be a conscious part of your time of intercession.

To pray consistently utilizing these noted principles will take the natural struggle out of prayer. Removing the unnecessary burdens makes the process of rising from the low place to a higher position easier. This makes it a joy to pray and not a chore to pray. It brings excitement! You will then make your appeals with expectation. Having hope and trust in whom you are communicating with, is key in seeing the results of your petitions.

It is also important to ask God for assistance in accepting His response be it "yes," "no", or "wait." I reiterate that the information presented to you in this reading is not a formula to be used to get what you want. These are spiritual strategies to bring you into agreement and alignment with the will of God to manifest what He wants. Why? Because His will is what is best! That said, as you ascend in prayer, you are equipped to handle heaven's response. Especially if the answer is "wait" or "no".

God is omniscient in that He is all-knowing, all-seeing, and all wise. He will acknowledge and reply to all prayers, even those that seem unanswered. It is we who must learn to accept and manage His responses. We dance and shout when He says "yes." When the response is "no" or "wait;" if not careful, disappointment becomes disillusionment. Disillusionment may lead to anger or distrust. Either can open the door for doubt, anxiety, loss of faith, and negative emotions. Negative emotions may lead to unwise choices or negative behaviors.

In waiting for the response to a prayer sent, we often do not listen for the "no" or the "wait." Often, the focus is on God's promises being "yes and amen" as if He never says "no." Know that He has and will give what appears to be an unfavorable response, particularly, when the request opposes His divine will. Evidence of this is noted in 2nd Samuel 12:14-23, which is the account of King David, who fasted and prayed for seven days for the life of his child conceived with Uriah's wife.

Although we read that King David was forgiven and his own life spared, it was not the case for his son. His son died despite the intense fasting and prayer on his behalf. Apostle Paul (2nd Cor. 12:7-9), was another who was given a thorn in the flesh. It caused him to pray not once, but three different times for it to be removed. God's response was, "My grace is sufficient." It is in the process of ascension that we are prepared to handle the Father's response.

Often, we want God to change the situation or the outcome. We seldom want to change our thinking, conversations, or behaviors. As we rise above the circumstances and whatever the associated feelings may be, God can then influence the heart. He can bring the mind and will into alignment with His plans and purposes. He is always concerned about what you are going through. Even more, He is concerned about your response to your issues, and your response to His reply.

King David and the Apostle Paul provide examples of the proper response when you do not get what you think you need or want. King David washed and anointed himself, worshipped, and then ate. Apostle Paul choose to delight in his own weakness for it was indicative of the strength and power of Christ, at work, in and around him. Both accepted God's perfect will over their own personal desires. We, too, must learn to embrace the will of God, and grow beyond just sending up a grocery list of what we want.

Learn how to remain committed to the call as a disciple (follower). Do not throw a tantrum or walk away from God when His response does not come when or how you think it should. Beyond your itemized checklist, the Father wants your heart. Just as you enjoy the aroma of fresh morning coffee or freshly picked flowers, so does the Father enjoy the fragrance of your prayers.

FRAGRANCE OF PRAYER

Prayers release a fragrance of love, devotion, and worship. It brings great delight when you release your cares and express your appreciation to Him. It is noted in Psalms 141:2 (part a): "Let my prayer be set forth as incense before you." Incense was and is commonly used during times of meditation and reflection. In biblical times, incense was extensively used in worship. Biblical history notes that God gave Moses detailed instructions for an extremely specific mixture of fragrant spices to be used only for the altar of incense.

The incense was made of pure spices of equal amounts. It was carefully prepared, and then kindled with fire to release a pleasant aroma that was reverently presented to God (See Exodus 30). The burning of this incense was done continuously. In the same way, we are to pray without ceasing. We are to engage in the recurring exchange of information and truths with God. The lingering, pleasant scent from the smoke of the altar of incense was carried upward symbolizing how the prayers of the righteous would go up before God as a sweet fragrance. Likewise, it is so today when we release heart-felt prayers from the altar of our hearts.

It is the pleasing, aromatic scent of the prayers of the faithful that surround the throne of God. This sentiment is captured in Rev. 8:3-4: "And another angel came and stood at the altar, having a golden censer; and there was given unto him much incense that he should offer it with the prayers of all saints upon the golden altar which was before the throne. And the smoke of the incense, which came with the prayers of the saints, ascended up before God out of the angel's hand."

This is the fragrance that goes up and hovers around the throne of God. Humble and righteous supplications that are effectual, fervent, without ill-intent, or manipulation. It is not the number of words, their rhythmic flow, or the length of the petition that makes it fragrant and acceptable to God. What causes the Father to welcome the daily requests and earnest pleas of the soul, is the sacrificial work of Jesus. Scented with the Holiness and Righteousness of Christ, your prayers are pleasing unto God.

Imperfect vessels can offer up perfect prayers, in Christ, by His Spirit. Just as Christ, our mediator, is at the right hand of the Father continually interceding for all. We, too, are to fill heaven with the fragrance of prayer. It serves as a reminder that we are praying in the earth.

Our coming to God is a sign of our reliance, trust, and total dependence upon Him. When you draw near to God, He will draw near to you. You must draw near first. Well, it seems you are making the first move. He made the first move with the giving of His only Son. You shift to advance toward Him because He has the answers to your questions. He has and is the solution to all problems. Drawing near to God elevates your focus from the problem below to the resolution above.

Ascension is not just about going up to reach God, but it is also about moving toward what you believe about God. You cannot stay where you are and expect things to change. Change happens when things are set in motion. To experience life, there must be movement. Your conversations and life activities will make known who or what you believe in. It is stated in James 2:26 that "For as the body without the spirit is dead, so faith without works is dead also." An action or series of actions must accompany your faith, as that leads to transformation, reformation, and manifestation.

Jesus said, "Come to me all ye that labor and are heavy laden" (Matt. 11:28). If you believe what you are praying, then move toward God. If you trust God to answer, then draw near to Him. Your sonship allows you to go directly to the place where God operates from, His throne. How do we get there? The assured way is in relationship with Him and ascension in prayer.

I remind you again, these principles are not presented as some magical concoction. However, consistent utilization of these guidelines will take the toil out of prayer. It makes talking to God much easier. Can you imagine, being in a relationship and never having consistent two-way dialogue with your mate? That union, most likely, will not be fruitful, and will not last long. Without a prescribed regimen when praying, it can become a burden. It is the loads of life that make ascension difficult, if not impossible.

These principles, as taught by Jesus, to His disciples, were not just something He said. They were given to remove the weight. Their purpose is to bring awareness that this is not just something you haphazardly do. This is a lifestyle. Making this a lifestyle also helps you to know God is not some distant, far-off source. He is a Present Help to navigate you through your obstacle course of life, so that He may ultimately raise you up. Remember, there are somethings that you will never know or experience in the low place.

Let us hear or read in this case, the conclusion of the whole matter. The overall intent of prayer is to usher us into a place, in God, that symbolizes our eternal state of spending eternity with Him. In Ascension, we are caught up or brought up to meet and commune with Him. The time is coming when the struggles, waiting, and labor of prayer will cease. We will forever be present with God. Then, there will be no need for the kinds of prayer we do today. There will no longer be the need to petition Him to do something or give something.

POSITIONED IN PRAYER

All things hidden will be revealed. All things broken will be fixed. All things needed will be provided. While we remain in the earth, we must not only pray to petition God for something; we must also pray to position ourselves in the consistent building of relationship with God that will forever stand. Our desire should not be just for what is in God's hand. That only satisfies temporarily. We must desire to reach the eternal place where we are forever in His presence.

In His presence, there is no need to ask for anything, because everything is already provided. In His presence is the fullness of joy with nothing lacking, missing, or broken. We want to enter and dwell in the place of rest. The place where there is no need to ask Him to come, heal, deliver, provide, or protect. The kingdom belongs to Him. Heaven is coming to earth, and earth is to come together with heaven. There is something coming that is far greater than what we presently know or have. Are you ready?

Well guess what? You do not have to wait. You can ascend! To do so, you must skillfully use the word of God. In God's word is the law for ascension. In His word, you can get a glimpse of what is to come. I assure you, just one momentary glance at what is to come will shift your focus from what is here in the earth to what is in heaven.

Remember, we are to set our affections on things above (Col. 3:2). We are to desire the eternal more than the now, and more than what is natural. Through the process of ascension, we can reach our final destination to stand forever in the presence of the Holy God. Then, we will be like Him, and we will see Him as He is (1 John 3:2). What joy to know that our communication with the Holy Father will transcend from prayers of petition to proclamations of eternal praise.

NOW IS THE TIME TO ASCEND
IN JESUS' NAME, AMEN!

SIGNPOST:

FROM TEST TO TESTIMONY

My heart overflows with joy, because as I was nearing the end of this ministry assignment, God gave miraculous and undeniable validation (signpost) for this work, through the following true testimony.

My many years of driving, as a bus operator while employed at the Chicago Transit Authority (CTA), afforded me the opportunity to meet a lot of interesting people. In fact, I could write books on the various types of people, and the wide range of experiences I encountered over the past 20 plus years. With that said, I was fortunate to meet a young man, and we quickly became good friends. We had the opportunity to meet, because he and his family owns and operates a catering truck in the downtown area of Chicago, near the hospital.

For 30 plus years, they have sold sandwiches and various kinds of foods. Due to their location, they had a large clientele. They were well-known, and above all, well-respected. On many occasions, I would stop and not only get good food, but my friend and I would share good conversation. We talked about a variety of subjects, especially spirituality.

He is a Christian, who emphatically believes that Jesus is Lord! He loves the Lord, and consistently demonstrated that through the care of the people he served. He not only provided food, but he had a listening ear. He was always willing to help. He possessed a servant's heart, and always had words to encourage the soul!

Working as early as I did, I would have quite an appetite after operating the bus up and down the street. I looked forward to the good food. More importantly, I looked forward to the fellowship that grew stronger over the years. My friend is positive proof that iron sharpens iron.

2020, the year that was ushered in with great revelations and promises of being a great year! If anyone would have told me on 1/1/2020 that by March we would be experiencing a national health crisis, I would not have believed it. I may have told them they were paranoid, and in need of a psychiatric evaluation. Sadly, we are living through the pandemic known as COVID-19, an infectious flu-like illness.

As a result of the highly infectious nature of this virus, it spread rapidly. Because of its unpredictable and deadly outcomes across the nations, many state officials called for everyone to stay home. We were advised to go out only when necessary. Only essential businesses were permitted to continue operating. But things like sports, various forms of entertainment, and restaurant dining was brought to a screeching halt; at least initially. Additionally, schools were temporarily closed, and churches were asked not to gather in large numbers.

With limited things to do, that of course significantly impacted the activity and mobility of the people. The pandemic negatively affected all areas of the economy, locally and nationally. For my friend, the stay-at-home order reduced his clientele to zero, which meant no income. Although he was still near the hospital, fear and uncertainty kept the essential hospital workers from patronizing his business.

Day after day, he would get up and prepare the truck and the food. Rarely would he conduct any business. Daily he was losing money, causing his wife to question him. She often asked why he would continue to waste time and resources. I will never forget the day, a Monday, I noticed my friend looked extremely discouraged. It was a light driving day for me, so I stopped the bus. I went to encourage my brother.

GOD WILL PROVIDE

I told him that even in the middle of this crisis, God was going to take care of him. God would bless him, but he needed to continue to trust in the sovereignty of God. I encouraged him to not focus on the loss of business. Instead, focus on the one who had sustained the business for over 30 years. Trust is easy when things are going well. I urged him, in the middle of experiencing a sudden loss of income, with no immediate solution, to trust God for the support of his family.

He listened and agreed. Yet, I still saw the concern in his eyes. On Tuesday as I drove by, I noticed there was still no activity, and no significant change in his circumstances, or his countenance. Wednesday, it was the same. Thursday, I did not go by his location. On Friday, something was different....

As I drove up, I saw him with his hands raised, and he was praising God! I pulled over and got off the bus. I walked over to him, praising the Lord with him. He did not see me at first, as his back was to me. When he turned and saw me, with an excitement in his voice and joy in his eyes that I had not seen all week, he said, "I have to tell you what happened on Thursday!"

He stated on Thursday, he woke up and prepared to conduct business as he always did. Once at his business site, still having had no customers, he leaned against his truck, looked upward, and began to pray. He spoke to the Lord and said, "I continue to buy food, prepare the food, and come down here but there are no customers. I continue to lose money. God, I need you to tell me what to do." He continued by saying to the Lord, "If you tell me to continue I will, but if you say don't continue; I won't."

THE RESULTS OF PRAYER

While praying, he heard a chirp, and noticed there was a sparrow on the ground with something in its mouth. At first, he was not sure what the sparrow had, but as he focused in on it, he discovered it was a dollar. The sparrow had a dollar bill in its mouth! The sparrow then dropped the dollar and stood over it.

Being led by the Holy Spirit, he moved toward the sparrow. The sparrow did not move.

He then reached down and picked up the dollar. The sparrow still did not move. Then he put the dollar in his pocket. He then felt compelled to walk over and get tortillas off his truck. Interestingly, the sparrow followed him. So, he broke the tortillas in pieces and threw them over the fence.

Immediately, many sparrows came and started eating. Then the word of the Lord came to him and said, "If I can send a sparrow with one dollar, surely I can sustain you at a time like this." Behind that word, a multitude of people started coming to buy food, just as the sparrows had suddenly shown up!

Through this unusual occurrence, God manifested His sustaining power! All of it happened as the result of prayer. What if he had not prayed? What if he had just accepted the circumstances and gave up? What if he had quit behind the questions and concerns of his wife? Sovereign God knew that my friend would pray and had everything in motion even before he prayed. God is omniscient and knows our thoughts even before we think them. He knows what is needed even before the request is made. Amid asking, God was already responding. That is how awesome God is!

I shared this testimony because I hope as you read it, you were able to identify several of the prayer principles discussed in this writing. No, these prayer guides are not to be used like a mystical mixture just to get what you want from God. These principles and strategies are designed to bring you into agreement and alignment with the will of the Lord. They are designed to bring you to a place of absolute trust in God to know that "all things (no matter how tragic) work together for good to them that love God, to them who are the called according to His purpose" (Rom. 8:28).

It is in His divine and perfect will that your needs are met, and you experience the desires of your heart. Therefore, "Delight yourself in the LORD, and He will give you the desires of your heart." (Psalm 37:4, Berean Study Bible)

Consistently commune with God in prayer. Ask the Holy Spirit to help you effectively incorporate these principles in your daily living. Make the fulfillment of God's will your priority. Live to give life to others, as Christ gave Life to you. Then, you will see His kingdom come and His will be done on earth and in your life, as it is already done in heaven!

ASCENSION:

GOD'S INTENTION FOR PRAYER

ABOUT THE AUTHOR

Lawrence "Deon" Hill has a Bachelor of Arts in Biblical Studies from Clement of Alexandria Theological Academy. He also studied for five years with Aactev8 International under the leadership of Dr. Adonijah Ogbonnaya. He is a highly sought-after motivational speaker, educator, and relationship coach with an unquenchable love and passion for the word of God. Well-known for his revelatory insight, wisdom, and exceptional ability to bring understanding of the scriptures, he has traveled the states sharing the heart, mind, and will of God.

He is a visionary, teacher, and counselor who is the founder and organizer of Consuming Fire Kingdom Ministries, a non-denominational fellowship in Chicago, Illinois, whose mission is to worship the God of excellence in excellence and to improve the quality of life for all humanity through the ministry work of reconciliation and restoration.

Lawrence Deon Hill also provides apostolic oversight to three other ministries. He consistently works diligently to fulfill his personal mandate to teach and train leaders. As an expositor of the gospel, he has recurring appearances on a variety of television, radio, educational, and other social media forums. For Lawrence Deon Hill, prayer is an integral part of his daily life that has produced the evidence of truth found in the principles of the model prayer that Jesus taught. Through the transformational power of prayer, as he continues to grow in the grace and knowledge of our Lord, so does his zeal to enlighten, empower, and unify all nations!

Lawrence Deon Hill and his wife, Antoinette, currently reside in Surprise, Arizona. They are the proud parents of two adult daughters (Arianna and Keyonna), and four grandchildren.

Contact the author at <u>cfkministries247@gmail.com</u>

Printed in the United States
by Baker & Taylor Publisher Services